Reinventing Leadership

Also by Warren Bennis:

Leaders: The Strategies for Taking Charge
Why Leaders Can't Lead
On Becoming a Leader
Beyond Bureaucracy: Essays on the Development and Evolution
  of Human Organization
An Invented Life: Reflections on Leadership and Change
Learning to Lead: A Workbook on Becoming a Leader
Beyond Leadership: Managing in the New Paradigm
Warren Bennis Executive Briefing Series

Also by Robert Townsend:

Up the Organization
Further up the Organization
The B² Chronicles

Reinventing Leadership

Strategies to Empower the Organization

Warren Bennis and Robert Townsend

William Morrow and Company, Inc.
New York

It is the policy of William Morrow and Company, Inc., and its imprints and affiliates, recognizing the importance of preserving what has been written, to print the books we publish on acid-free paper, and we exert our best efforts to that end.

Library of Congress Cataloging-in-Publication Data

Bennis, Warren G.
    Reinventing leadership: strategies to empower the organization / Warren Bennis and Robert Townsend.—1st ed.
       p.   cm.
    ISBN 0–688–12670–7
    1. Leadership. 2. Decentralization in management. I. Townsend, Robert, 1920–   . II. Title.
    HD57.7.B465   1995
    658.4'092—dc20   95–7685
                                                                          CIP

Printed in the United States of America

First Edition

3   4   5   6   7   8   9   10

BOOK DESIGN BY SUSAN HOOD

Contents

Introduction

Making the transition from the old style of leadership to the new one is a challenge for top management at every organization. The militaristic, command-and-control leadership of the past has become an anachronism. In the post-downsizing, flat-management era today, a new leadership style is necessary. The time has come to ask yourself: Have you and your company adapted to this new set of standards or are you hanging on to the anachronistic rules of the past?

In Reinventing Leadership, *we discuss some of the ideas that help define this notion of new leadership. We address questions such as: What are some of the characteristics a new leader must have? What was wrong with the old ways of doing things? How does one become a new leader in one's own right? Then, using dialogue form, we attempt to arrive at a better understanding of what direction leadership is taking in today's corporation.*

As you follow along, see if there are any questions that come to your mind and that might be pertinent to address in your own organization. Included after each section are dialogue starters. These exercises are meant to stimulate further discussion between you and your co-workers. In most cases, you will need another person to engage in these leadership dialogues, and, in some cases, a dialogue group is recommended. You also might want to record your sessions for further use. Use these exercises as a means to gain further insight into your organization's problems and policies. You can try picking different partners and see what new issues might develop. Remember to keep yourself open to new possibilities and to stay away from pat answers. In this way you can gain a new understanding of how to reinvent some of your own methods of leadership.

—WARREN BENNIS AND ROBERT TOWNSEND

Reinventing Leadership

Chapter 1

Reinventing the Leader

Who personifies the leader of today? Being in charge doesn't necessarily have the same connotations of "absolute power" that it used to have. In fact, today's leaders find themselves benefiting from a more collaborative approach to management. By checking their egos at the door, so to speak, leaders will find that they can tap into endless sources of potential from the people they lead.

Today's business climate calls for a new definition of what it takes to make an organization run. With rapidly changing technology, a downsized work force, and an emphasis on acquiring a broad range of skills, leaders today have to be more flexible than ever in their roles. Taking risks in their approach to management is the only choice left for those who want to have an impact on an increasingly global work force.

This chapter gives you an introduction to some of the basic ideas Robert Townsend and I have regarding the changing role of leadership in today's environment. Understanding some of the initial, broad-based principles every good leader should apply might illuminate for you some of the major mistakes made in the corporation today. As we delve more deeply into the techniques and strategies that constitute effective leadership, you'll begin to get a clearer picture of why leadership must always be a complex blend of art and science.

—WARREN BENNIS

What's wrong with the old style of leadership?

Townsend: Let me state a basic old form of leadership. This anachronism is the person who in effect says to his organization, "I order all of you insignificant little people to come to work excited, energetic, and creative and to accomplish impossible tasks, so that I may become rich and famous and live a luxurious life traveling around the world and building a home on the Riviera and playing golf with other important people like myself. By the way, I want you to park in the outer lot and slog through the snow past the empty parking space with my name on it, and I also want you to pay for your coffee while I get mine free, served on fine china."

That was the old model, and it worked. Some great companies were built, and they prospered with that kind of leader. But now we're a long way past that.

Bennis: You have to wonder why it worked, when it worked, and why it doesn't work today. In a marvelous old movie called *Twelve O'Clock High,* the command-and-control model of leadership is represented by Gregory Peck taking over this demoralized battalion and revitalizing it. It's a continuation of the myth of the great man.

But we've got to go from macho to maestro, from someone who thinks he has all the answers and gets all the perks to someone who can conduct his staff to find its own answers. The old style is just not going to work anymore. It probably worked for a little while because it embodies bureaucracy and one-person control. That notion of bureaucracy was perfect for an environment that was predictable and orderly. The reason leaders of this type succeeded was because they could forecast what was going to happen in two years.

Townsend: Just a minute, Warren. Calling people "staff" isn't much better than calling them subordinates or employees. By now we ought to be better at thinking of people as associates or colleagues or partners, and calling them that. But why don't you think command-and-control will work today?

Bennis: Because today we live in an environment in which technology is changing the way we think. Today, demography is destiny and the world gives us vertigo every day as we read the newspaper. With globalization and a whole new world order, I don't see how the old type of leadership could work today.

Townsend: Come on, get specific. Why won't it work?

Bennis: Here's why, Bob. The key to competitive advantage in the 1990s and beyond will be the capacity of leadership to create a social architecture capable of generating intellectual capital. The key words in that dense sentence are the last two. Intellectual capital means ideas, know-how, innovation, knowledge, and expertise. That's what's going to make the difference. Restructuring and reengineering can take you only so far; you cannot restructure or reengineer your company into prosperity. That takes ideas and reinvention. And reinvention takes, as I said, brains and ideas and knowledge. You're not going to attract or retain a work force like that under silly and obsolete forms of bureaucratic, command-and-control leadership. You can't release the brainpower of any organization by using whips and chains. You get the best out of people by empowering them, by supporting them, by getting out of their way. As author Max De Pree said, you've got to abandon your ego to the talents of others. That's why.

Townsend: Great leaders are like great presidents. A number of years ago, I asked this question of Robert Sobel, a history teacher and author: "When are we going to get great leaders in this country?" Sobel looked me straight in the eye and replied, "Hopefully not in my lifetime. Great leaders inevitably take the United States over the precipice."

Bennis: I think a great president, like any other great leader, has to have at least three things. First, a strong set of convictions. Second, a devoted constituency. Third, the capacity to use his position as a bully pulpit to muster broad support for his goals. These criteria are what leaders need at the national level, and this vision is what organizations need at the local level.

Bureaucracies, on the other hand, really don't encourage leadership. The best institutions are those that grow leaders, and that requires a totally different view of what organizations should be like.

Townsend: I'll give you those three, but I'm glad you said "at least." For me, the first quality a president needs is character. Then experience, intelligence, and energy are necessary. From those come the strong set of convictions. Don't worry—the bully pulpit and the devoted constituency will follow.

Dialogue Starters

1. ROLE-PLAYING DIALOGUE: You and your partner take different sides in a debate—one of you defends the command-and-control leader; the other attacks that leadership style. Stay away from the personalities of people in your company, instead focusing on the traits and prototype of a command-and-control leader.

2. PARTNER ANALYSIS: You and your partner each take turns evaluating the other's tendencies toward command-and-control traits. Defend yourself if you don't believe you possess a given trait or if you feel it is a positive rather than a negative.

3. GROUP DIALOGUE: Secure the participation of between three and five people for a group discussion. The topic: whether your CEO possesses the three ideal "presidential" traits—a strong set of convictions, a devoted constituency, and the ability to use her office as a bully pulpit. Appoint one member of the group as a leader with responsibility for controlling the dialogue, keeping it on the subject at hand, and avoiding domination of the group by any one member.

What's the difference between managing and leading?

Townsend: It always seemed that I worked at about 20 percent of capacity when I was working for a manager, and it was largely because I didn't feel free to act; I had to wait for permission or for decisions to be made by others. Or I was afraid to take the chance of making a mistake. When I worked for a *leader,* I was excited, free, more creative, more energetic, unafraid, and I worked at 80 percent of capacity.

Bennis: Here's another way to define the difference: Leaders are people who do the right things and managers are people who do things right. Leaders are interested in direction, vision, goals, objectives, intention, purpose, and effectiveness—the right things. Managers are interested in efficiency, the how-to, the day-to-day, the short run of doing things right.

Townsend: And not making mistakes. You also work *for* a manager, while you work *with* a leader. A manager tends to think of his people in terms of how much they cost and how little he can pay them. A leader tends to think of his people as resources and wonders how much they can earn and how he can help them become heroes.

Bennis: I once created a whole list of distinctions between manager and leader; some of the following might prove helpful.

- The manager administers; the leader innovates.
- The manager is a copy; the leader is an original.
- The manager maintains; the leader develops.

- The manager focuses on systems and structure; the leader focuses on people.
- The manager relies on control; the leader inspires trust.
- The manager has a short-term view; the leader has a long-term view.
- The manager asks why and how; the leader asks what and why.
- The manager has her eye on the bottom line; the leader has her eye on the horizon.

Bennis: It's very clear to me that failing organizations almost always fail because they're overmanaged and they're underled.

Townsend: I think we have to make a distinction between being a manager and performing your managerial duties effectively. It's not that leaders don't have anything to do with management. There is no reason why a good leader can't handle the finer aspects of the job, even the more mundane detail work, occasionally.

Bennis: Right. I strongly disagree with those who believe leaders and managers are utterly distinct psychological types, and that if you're one you can't be the other. The very best leaders do care about detail, about the grunge work.

The reason, however, I'm emphasizing the distinction is that leaders are the only ones capable of creating a culture where people feel valued, where they're energized, where they're creative, where they love coming to work, where work is "more fun than fun," to quote Noel Coward.

Townsend: How many leaders do you know who have a problem with also being a follower? When we're talking about leaders, we should also mention the importance of being a follower.

Bennis: Good leaders should also be good followers. If you're coming up within an organization, you must be a good follower or you're not going to get very far. Leaders and followers share certain characteristics such as listening, collaborating, and working out competitive issues with peers. I made a major mistake in naming my books *Leaders, Why Leaders Can't Lead,* and *On Becoming a Leader.* I should have called them *Followers, Why Followers Can't Follow,* and *On Becoming a Follower.*

Townsend: I agree with that. What ambitious junior executive wants to get caught by his colleagues reading *On Becoming a Leader?* If you want to determine whether you're working for a leader rather than a manager, ask yourself these questions:

- Do you work *with* your boss or *for* your boss?
- Do you have specific targets?
- Do you have enough power and resources to hit your targets?
- Do you get enough feedback on how you're doing?
- Does your boss protect you from useless work, pointless interruptions, ridiculous committees, memoranda, and paperwork?
- Are you coming to work excited, full of energy, free to make mistakes and fail?
- Do you feel "zap-proof," or free from punishment for your mistakes?

Bennis: I'd like to add to your list:

- Do you feel significant at work?
- Do you think you do anything important or meaningful?
- Do you feel, in other words, that you're at the center of things rather than on the periphery of things?
- Are you learning anything?
- Is your environment educational, a place where people claim they learn more than in graduate school?
- Do you feel you're part of the community or the group?
- Do you feel you belong?
- Are the rewards you receive based on performance?
- Do you feel pride in your organization?

Dialogue Starters

1. MANAGEMENT EVALUATION: On a piece of paper, answer the questions provided above and determine whether you work for a manager or a leader. Compare notes with your partner.

2. DEBATE QUESTIONS: Do you believe leaders should also be good followers, or are the two sets of traits incompatible? Can someone effectively combine the characteristics of both managers and leaders?

How does someone become a leader?

Townsend: If I were reading this and I were a middle manager, I'd think of my opportunity this way: I'm not going to make any speeches or write any memos, but I'm just going to start acting like a leader and see what happens. If people who work with me become excited and energetic and creative, I'm going to become a hero as a result of their efforts. As long as I remember to thank them, I'm going to be on my way.

Bennis: This strategy could work, but there are environments in which you can't behave this way—then you have to take chances or even leave. You should realize that organizations don't always realize they're blocking leadership behaviors. I hear many executives asking, "Why don't these people [employees] take the initiative? We've unlocked the doors for them. They just have to open them up." The point is that not only employees but executives have to adjust to a new leadership environment. Executives must be the social architects and reward the behaviors we've discussed.

But don't wait for Godot if you're a middle manager. Don't wait for someone to say, "Go ahead, be a leader." If this stuff makes sense to you, take the first step, take the risk.

Townsend: Just make up your mind about what you're going to do and do it. Take risks, make mistakes, take the blame. Identify the goal of your part of the organization— what you want to become compared to what you are. Then fight to make sure your people get rewarded and they make changes that achieve the goal. Keep your head down and have fun. If you're careful that your people receive the credit for what you've done or what they've accomplished under your guidance, you'll receive a tap on the shoulder someday and somebody will say, "Hey, we have a problem over in this area. Would you like to take it over?" You'll have several people ready to step into your shoes, because your behavior has helped grow new leaders.

Bennis: It's a new world, that's the essence of it. To quote my favorite management philosopher, Yogi Berra, "The future ain't what it used to be." We expect new kinds of behaviors and values from our leaders if they want to make it in the twenty-first century. Changes in technology, demographic diversity, and globalization will require our leaders to be more articulate, energetic, and empowering than ever before. The things that made them successful ten years ago are not the things that will make them successful today and tomorrow.

Dialogue Starters

1. DEBATE QUESTION: Assume people in your organization took our suggestion and started acting like leaders—how do you think management would respond? You take the stance that management would be delighted and would respond positively; your partner should argue for a negative response, perhaps because management would be worried about controlling so many independent-minded leaders.

2. PARTNER ANALYSIS: Take turns evaluating each other's willingness to, in Robert Townsend's words, "take risks, make mistakes, take the blame." If either of you finds the other reluctant to do these things, is the problem internal ("I'm afraid to take risks"), external ("Management will punish me for taking risks"), or a combination of both?

3. WHAT-IF DISCUSSION: If you were to be transferred or fired or you otherwise left your position suddenly, would there be a leader available to succeed you? If not, why not? If there would be one, evaluate the candidate for leadership skills previously discussed.

Chapter 2

Developing the Traits of a Leader

No two leaders are alike. That's because leadership comes in many different forms: Leaders are left-brained and right-brained, dressed for success and improperly dressed. They vary in their management philosophies and have distinct personality quirks. But one idea remains significant—that leadership is unique to each person. Neither science nor formula will produce a leader; leadership is a matter of character.

In this chapter, we'll define some of the paradoxical characteristics and attitudes that combine to form the personality of an effective leader. We'll also talk about some of the techniques you can use to empower and develop your employees. These are essentially people skills, and you probably possess most of them, to some degree. Think about your leadership setting and how growing in these areas might help your personal transformation as a leader.

—ROBERT TOWNSEND

What does it take to be a leader?

Townsend: There are a number of characteristics that a good leader must possess. I guess the first on my list would be the notion of personal ambition under control. And yet, I don't see it on anybody else's list. I'm sure that directors don't consider that when they're selecting the new CEO.

Bennis: I think George Shultz's testimony before a Senate committee during the Iran-Contra scandal brilliantly sums it up, because he was honest and simple and because he distinguished himself. He was one of the few people who didn't get their hands dirtied in that situation. At the very end of his testimony, Senator Daniel Inouye, the chairman of the committee, said to him, "Look, we thank you for being here and sharing your views with us. Do you have any advice for the American public?" And he said, "Yes, just remember one thing, Senator. Don't give power to people who can't live without it."

Townsend: The second characteristic is intelligence and the third is the ability to be articulate. I don't think they necessarily go together and I don't even mean that either one has to be extraordinary. But certainly, a leader must be adequately intelligent and adequately articulate.

Bennis: The more I think about what institutions require, the more I think that good-enough intelligence and a superb ability to be articulate are critical. I don't know how we get intelligence, but I think we can learn how to improve our communicating ability, which is part of what you're talking about.

Townsend: Exactly. The English language is a minefield. And if you're writing memos, you can't see the mines go off—that's why communicating eyeball-to-eyeball is so important.

Bennis: I want to give you three very specific examples of the importance of communication. During the Tylenol scandal and disaster in 1982, when some lunatic put cyanide into Tylenol capsules, Jim Burke at Johnson and Johnson was actually able to improve the market share of Tylenol. He was able to articulate the problem to the public and was very open and candid about it. Without his capacity to really be a spokesman for that company, I think it would have been a total disaster.

Second, Jack Welch, Jr., at General Electric is really transforming that organization. He is spending an enormous amount of time in workout groups throughout the country. And, in his own words, he spends his time eyeball-to-eyeball, working not through video, not through pronouncements, but traveling to different offices relentlessly. To the point where I don't know how much longer he can keep up the pace.

Or look at Max De Pree, innovative former CEO of the furniture company Herman Miller, Inc., and author of the books *Leadership Jazz* and *Leadership Is an Art*. He is also an example of a man who is capable of putting words to goals, of actually articulating his mission. I can't exaggerate the significance of being able to communicate well, although you rarely see it on a list of criteria when people select new leaders. Given the blurry world we live in, given its ambiguities, it's really important for the leader to be able to speak clearly, simply, and articulately.

Townsend: The next point I want to make about a good leader is that he must be a servant to his people. The overly ambitious, power-craving, insensitive types don't make good leaders because they don't understand this role. But as Max De Pree says, most of the time he's a servant to his people, making sure that they don't have any reason to fail, that their wants are fulfilled, and that they have every resource they need to achieve their targets.

Bennis: This point fits in very nicely with the first point you made about people—don't give power to people who want it too much. Because I think the people who want it too much also want the trappings. They want the limousines, the private jets, the entourages; they want all the perks, the props of power. As Max De Pree put it, "The first task of a leader is to define reality. The last task is to say 'thank you,' and in between he's a servant." I think that's a tough thing to do.

Townsend: The servant role is not a continuous one. If, for instance, the CEO is the principal new-business getter of an organization, then when he is working on getting a new contract or a new client, he needs to act like an emperor. Everybody on his staff has to support him and bring him cups of coffee and whatever else he needs to get that job done. But once that job is achieved and nailed down, he goes back to his servant role. I would expand the servant concept to say that there is also an emperor role, as well as cheerleader, coach, and whatever other roles you want to give, played by the leader.

The next characteristic a leader must possess is objectivity. He must be someone who is constantly referring back to his mission when problems come up. Someone who makes all his decisions based not on what he had for breakfast or how he feels or whether he likes the person he's dealing with, but on whether it gets him closer to this vision or backs him off. That's what I mean by objectivity.

Bennis: I don't know if I would call it objectivity. I think *purpose* is a better word. The thing I found out about most good leaders is that they do have a positive self-regard and often not too big an ego.

Townsend: You mean an absence of arrogance.

Bennis: Right. But they do have to have a strong ego, strong enough to take the abuse, strong enough to handle the kind of anger you'll sometimes incur, and yet also strong enough to appreciate contrary feedback from other people.

Dialogue Starters

1. GROUP DIALOGUE: Assess your own leaders in your organization in terms of ambition, intelligence, and objectivity. What about the ability to communicate and to be a servant to employees? Are there any other traits you admire in the leaders you presently work with that should be included on this list? What about people who are overly ambitious or power hungry? Do you think those who are in a position of power need their own set of checks and balances? How can you ensure that they are not so isolated that they can't be reined in when their need for control becomes too great? How about making sure there is always a reliable, fearless, ambitionless sounding board? What sorts of checks and balances are there at your place of business? How can they be improved?

2. PARTNER ANALYSIS: Evaluate the ability of your partner to communicate as a leader. Pinpoint which messages get communicated and which ones don't. Can you find new ways of communicating more successfully? Take turns demonstrating how you would tell someone in your de-

partment that he was doing something incorrectly and needed to modify his approach. Now each person should try to write it in memo form. Compare and contrast the two different approaches. Which is more effective? How does personality come into play on the part of the communicator? On the part of the listener? Suppose the error is being committed upstairs? Does the information get passed up the chain quickly, or does it just get to some weak link and then get swept under the rug?

Where can leaders go wrong?

Townsend: One way that leaders can go wrong is by taking all the credit. A good leader is someone who never takes credit. This trait is high on my list. It's been my experience that the people who gain trust, loyalty, excitement, and energy fast are the ones who pass on the credit to the people who really have done the work. A leader doesn't need any credit; he's already in the top slot. He's getting more credit than he deserves anyway. I think it's essential that he pass on all the credit he can to the rest of the organization.

Bennis: I think this goes along with the notion of mentoring, learning to help your people grow and allowing them to reap the rewards of work that's done well.

Townsend: Mentoring is wonderful when it is going on, but it thrives only in a fearless environment. In the chilly climate of downsizing and restructuring, when people are afraid of losing their jobs, mentoring breaks down. Another casualty is the sense of humor, of having fun in the office. I don't think I've ever run into a leader who didn't have a good sense of humor that seemed to get better when times got tough. Yet I don't see humor on any lists.

Bennis: I think it's very important. Before writing my last book, I consulted with a friend of mine who was a gag writer for Bob Hope and Johnny Carson. He's been writing gags for years, and I wanted him to instruct me on developing a sense of humor and also on joke telling. I paid my friend something like a hundred dollars an hour for six months until he finally decided I was hopeless. Along with honesty, we all think we possess a sense of humor. And we know from experience that it just isn't true. But I think humor is extremely important. I'm not sure how you learn it, how you get it. But if you have a sense of humor, that means you are detached enough from a situation, you have enough distance from it to be able to laugh at yourself. The best humor is when you can reframe an issue and take it from a win/lose situation to something that clarifies and illuminates.

Townsend: George Meredith called it "the comic spirit," the ability to laugh at things even when they're painful. He thought it was humanity's saving grace. It's somehow connected with humility, with the absence of arrogance, which is why it's comforting if a leader possesses it.

Bennis: It's been said that "integrity and wisdom are essential to success in business. Integrity means when you promise a customer something, keep that promise, even if you lose money. And wisdom is: Don't make such promises!" Humor can definitely tide you over during those rough times.

Townsend: For a leader to be effective, that person must be "inclusive." I say this based on my experience as a follower. I remember several bosses who, when anything really interesting or significant or powerful in the way of information or visitors or personalities came into the organization, would hoard them jealously. Even though their followers would have benefited more from contact with them than the bosses would. By inclusive, I mean the ability to know when your followers will benefit from learning some idea or meeting some person and to make sure that they do.

Bennis: It's a word used by a lot of people concerned with the issue of embracing diversity, which is an inclusionary thing. It's saying, let's bring more voices in, let's talk to diverse sets of people we haven't talked to in the past, and let's share—let's be more open. One of my favorite phrases is "reflective backtalk,"[1] which means being able to reflect on your experiences. Using others' input to discuss past successes and failures, future projects, and how to make things better is one of the most effective means of learning.

Townsend: One way to encourage reflective backtalk is to put on a dog-and-pony show for your colleagues and associates about a new product or service or strategy before it's too late to change or abort it. If you welcome criticism, they'll realize you want feedback and reality checks and they'll open up.

Bennis: That helps to create a more collegial, team-oriented workplace, and gets the leader the kind of consensus he needs to execute a new program.

Townsend: Another important characteristic a leader needs to develop is toughness. And by that I mean someone who protects his people. Tough against the impingement of outside interruptions and outside burdens. In my case, I can't tell you how many times I had to do work in the early

1. Thanks to Don Michael for this idea.

part of my career that I knew was pointless, that required a lot of energy and a lot of people-hours, and that was assigned to me because my boss didn't have the toughness to say to his boss or to an outside director, "What on earth are you going to do with that information once we develop it? Do you really need that information? Let's discuss it and see if I can't answer it on the telephone." Instead, he'd say, "Yes sir, yes sir, I'll have Bob Townsend do that right away," which would mean I'd work Saturday and Sunday to prepare a useless memorandum. Resisting that is what I mean by tough.

Bennis: So it's really leader as protector. It's being able to stand up to your boss, too, and knowing how to handle the boss. That takes another kind of toughness.

Townsend: Being able to stand up to a powerful, uninformed outsider, which is not normally done in business. Jack Welch, Jr., may do it—I'm sure he does. But there are a whole lot of CEOs out there who do not stand up to powerful outside directors to protect their people. It's very valuable because, if you do it enough, the word gets all over the organization and helps build trust and loyalty.

Bennis: There have been studies that show that seven out of ten Americans are afraid to question their superiors. They won't speak up, even when they know those superiors are wrong and they could prevent the boss or the company from making a terrible mistake. I view leaders as social architects who must engineer an atmosphere in which creative dissent is welcomed and rewarded and people are willing to take risks.

Townsend: A leader must be fair. And fair is difficult. For example, most people, including leaders, tend to spend more time with people they like, and those people understandably, but unfairly, wind up with more opportunities to shine and more rewards for success. It takes a strong need for fairness to stay out of the crony trap, but it's worth the effort.

Dialogue Starters

1. LISTING EXERCISE: **Make a list of the things you would look for in a mentor. When was the last time you offered these same services to others? Can you think of different ways to mentor the people with whom you work?**

2. MANAGEMENT EVALUATION: **Write down the experiences you've had where someone has stood up to you and said no and vice versa. What did you gain from these experiences? If at times you weren't effective, what would you do differently? Have you ever let an issue pass even though you knew it would harm your company or your fellow employees? What were the consequences?**

3. BRAINSTORMING DIALOGUE: **Brainstorm a way for you and your company to receive "reflective backtalk" from others. Could it be in a formal meeting situation? In a communal memo? Through E-mail? A suggestion box? How effective is your company in communicating its progress to its employees? Think of new ways to broaden your inclusivity.**

What is the definition of executive character?

Bennis: The three traits that define executive character are like the legs of a tripod: No leg can stand without the others. One is ambition, the drive and need for power and achievement. Second is competence or expertise. Third is integrity, which includes authenticity and an external anchor.

Now let's do a little exercise. Imagine a person with just one of these traits. Someone with unbridled ambition would be a demagogue. A person who is only supercompetent would be a technocrat. Anyone who has integrity but lacks competence and drive would likely be a warm and fuzzy figure. Though, as Mae West once said, "Too much of a good thing can be wonderful." I think that too much integrity can be like that.

But the really terrific executive has a delicate balance of these three traits. Two of the traits are insufficient, though some people who get ahead in organizations possess competence and ambition. During times of change and turbulence—during mergers and acquisitions, for instance—these guys often get to the top. I call them destructive achievers. They have competence and ambition but lack integrity. They're the ones who create low trust in institutions.

Townsend: Warren, I can't go along with you on "ambition, the drive and need for power and achievement." That leg of a tripod tends to contract elephantiasis. Ambition rings warning bells in me, and when you add "need for power" my skin begins to crawl. I think I know what you mean, but do me a favor and let's start on the other side of the tripod. Integrity is 100 percent right. The word makes me think of every great coach, teacher, and leader I ever had. They could really bring out the best in all of us.

Your second leg, "competence or expertise," is a must also. Without it, the learning curve is too long and the timing is disrupted. Let me try to rename the third leg without weakening it. How about "an insatiable drive to help associates become heroes in the quest to reach the organization's goals''? That, it seems to me, is ambitious in the right way, and includes the need for achievement and the proper use of power. Maybe you can shorten my definition a little.

Dialogue Starters

1. PARTNER ANALYSIS: Evaluate each other's strengths and weaknesses regarding executive traits. Focus most of the discussion on any trait that is missing, and the negative impact (if any) on your or your partner's performance.

2. MANAGEMENT EVALUATION: Discuss whether you have any destructive achievers in top management positions and the negative (or positive) impact they've had. How has their lack of integrity manifested itself, and how do people react to it, both internally and externally?

What are some of the paradoxical traits a leader might possess?

Townsend: One of the most common paradoxes of leadership is that it requires both patience and urgency. When it comes to leadership, patience is an important characteristic. For example, a good leader agrees with me on my goal but doesn't take the job away from me several months later, when she's unhappy with my progress. In other words, a leader who has the patience to know that I'm going to make it—who encourages me and says, "What else do you need? What can I do to help?"

A sense of urgency, at times, is the other half of this paradox. Just saying "I'm not going to wait. I need it now.

Move it up your priority list" helps to ensure that the job gets done.

There's always a sensitive balance between the two that a leader must intuitively recognize. You've had a boss, I'm sure, who wanted something done tomorrow morning, only you were trying to do a really good job and it would take you a week. Because he had some director pressing him for it, and he couldn't see the difference, he forced you to rush the work and turn in something you neither understood nor believed in. He did a bad job but got it off his list. That's why patience is so important. Incorporating both sides of the paradox, to form what you might call "patient urgency," is perhaps one good way to lead.

The next paradox is that the leader needs to be available or visible so that people won't need him as much. That means that when somebody's working on a project and she gets to a brick wall and needs help getting over it or through it, she needs her leader. She needs to be able to walk through the door and say, "This is where I am, I want help getting on the other side of that wall." The opposite of available is the CEO who is on seven outside boards, does a lot of committee work, chairs the local hospital fund drive, and is just never there when needed.

The way a leader becomes available is that he gets his house in order. He gets the vision understood, agreed on, articulated, communicated, until everybody knows what the company or organization is trying to become. He structures the reward system so that it encourages progress toward that vision. He gets feedback going so that people can measure their progress toward that vision monthly or even more often.

Then control or administration is much less burden-some. Then he's got time. People don't come to him that often because they know what the goal is, they know what their power is, and they know how they're doing. It's not important for him to be around. That's the paradox.

Bennis: It's a balance that's almost impossible to achieve, though, Bob. You've either entrusted your people with so much power that it seems like they don't need you, or they resent you for not delegating enough and being ineffec-tive.

Townsend: Well, when it comes to problem solving, what's most important is that the leader be effective. You've heard about the boss who has a closed door and is not available. That's one way. Then there's the boss with the open door who's just delighted to hear about your problems and will listen all day, solve them for you, and go home feeling like God.

What *I* mean by effective is someone who makes *me* ef-fective by saying, "Before you go any further, you're giving me your problem. I hope it's accompanied by the best so-lution from where you sit. If it isn't, go back and work until you've got some suggestions on how to handle it, because I've got my own problems." Someone who, when I come in with good news that we don't need to act on, says to me, "Look, I appreciate the good news, but I'll read about that eventually in the profit-and-loss statement, so don't bother me with good news. Bother me with bad news." Setting that sort of limit is effective. You don't have to have more than a few of those meetings before your whole cadre becomes effective in that way.

Bennis: If I were to give a definition of leadership, which you and I have properly avoided because there are at least

650 of them in literature, it would be the capacity to create a compelling and plausible vision and to translate that vision into organizational realities.

Now if you take that as an overarching view of leadership, I think I would also include the ability to generate and sustain trust, and the ability to be agile and adaptive enough to changing situations. There are so many paradoxes and subtleties. Leadership, if nothing else, is a deeply nuanced thing. I don't think you and I, in struggling to look at the qualities of it, are recognizing that.

I also think that my list would include openness to diverse points of view. Openness to valid feedback, from as many sources as you can get. Because the more open to other people's viewpoints and the more active a listener you are, the better informed you're going to be as a leader.

Townsend: Hold on, Warren. You don't mean "as many sources as you can get"! One of the great characteristics of a leader is to know when to stop gathering data and pull the trigger. You and I have both suffered under people who used data gathering to postpone a badly needed decision.

Bennis: Well, decisiveness is an important factor, as well—knowing when it's time to make the decision. The final characteristic for me would be self-knowledge, self-awareness. It's true that the unexamined life is not worth living. I really believe that the best leaders I've met and known over the years have been reflective practitioners, that they both think and act. There's a lot of knowledge about how they affect other people, a lot of knowledge about themselves, a lot of knowledge about their strengths and weaknesses. That's what helps to make them the best.

Townsend: I like that very much. In my good bosses the self-knowledge showed up as not taking themselves too seriously. At the same time, they weren't afraid to admit their shortcomings. Those were bosses I trusted, and we all know the difference between working for someone you trust and someone you don't trust.

Dialogue Starters

1. GROUP DIALOGUE: Gather a group of people together and discuss the advantages and disadvantages of having a leader who solves problems for the company versus a leader who puts the problems back into the employees' hands. How can a leader maintain a company's vision without hands-on control at all times? How open is your workplace to communal problem solving? What if employees were to share problems weekly in a group atmosphere and not count on a leader's advice? Explore new techniques for problem solving.

2. PARTNER ANALYSIS: Have your partner help you determine which type of leader you are: someone who is often patient but perhaps a little too laid back, or perhaps someone who is able to communicate a sense of urgency but not able to wait for things to happen? Take turns role-playing a situation where someone who works for you can't seem to finish a project you've been waiting a month for. This person has trouble meeting deadlines and doesn't want any help finishing up his work. How can you get him to hurry up without demotivating him?

Chapter 3

The Personal Side of Leadership

Leaders communicate their vision to those around them in ways that emotionally enroll others to turn this vision into reality. One of the reasons followers are drawn to this "pragmatic dreamer" is because he or she makes them feel significant. But with influence comes responsibility, and a call for the leader's own house to be in order. He must have a strong sense of self-awareness and a desire for constant personal development. In this deeply personal business of leadership, you must be in the process of bringing out the best in yourself before you can bring out the best in your followers.

In this chapter, you'll learn how personal discovery can be the starting point for making an impact on your organization. You'll also discover ways to build positive self-regard by steadily nurturing your strengths, being aware of what the organization needs and expects from you, and inviting "reflective backtalk" at every opportunity. If yes-

terday's leader took reflective backtalk from only a few close associates, today's leader must maintain sensitivity to the views of everyone who has a stake in the company and realize that each one can make a special contribution to meeting the company's goals. When it comes to developing the personal characteristics that make a good leader, taking these actions will not only assist your personal growth, but will result in innovations and added productivity to your organization.

—WARREN BENNIS

What do you mean by "the personal side" of leadership?

Bennis: When I talk about the personal side of leadership, I want to talk about positive self-regard. To me, it is the most important and the most difficult issue to talk about. In a way, I'm talking about self-esteem, but I use the phrase "positive self-regard" because it is more descriptive.

Positive self-regard usually consists of three factors. The first is to know your strengths and weaknesses, which sounds very prosaic. I think that's very, very important, and a lot of people go through life without ever understanding themselves. And one of the things I've noticed about leaders is that earlier in their careers they identified what they were good at and what they were bad at, and tended to— how does Johnny Mercer's song go?—to accentuate the positive and to eliminate the negative. So they tend not to overlook the negative things, but to make their strengths effective and their weaknesses irrelevant. That's the first thing I'd say about positive self-regard.

Townsend: I like that: "Make their strengths effective and their weaknesses irrelevant."

Bennis: The second part of positive self-regard is that leaders allow themselves to develop many opportunities for nurturing their strengths through goal setting. They're like good athletes—they challenge themselves constantly. They also surround themselves with different ways of getting feedback on how they're doing. I think most good athletes, like most good leaders, need feedback to evaluate how far they are from their goals.

The third thing that I've noticed among effective leaders is that they understand the fit between what the institution requires and what they can contribute. People often refer to it as good timing, but it's far beyond good timing. Good timing sounds like luck. But what I found in my own analysis in the study of leaders, as well as my own experience, is that effective leaders know where their efforts will be best applied. In the first study I did of leaders a number of years ago—there were ninety leaders in this group—only two of them ever overstayed their time as CEO of their organizations.

Those two failed to understand that their particular talents were no longer appropriate for what those organizations needed and they were forced out by their boards.

Townsend: I see a strong correlation in leaders between competence and knowing when to retire. This is the deadliest factor in selecting a new leader. If the choice is wrong, the mistake will dig in and stay forever. And we know how reluctant boards of directors are to correct their errors.

Bennis: I noticed something else, which I had no way of accounting for, in that first study I did on leadership. Of those ninety leaders, sixty were on the corporate side, the other thirty on the public service or government side; forty of the sixty were in the Fortune 500. *Of those forty Fortune 500 CEOs, thirty-eight of them were still not only married to their first spouses, but wildly enthusiastic about the institution of marriage, which fascinated me.* I later went back to talk to some of those forty and I said, "Look, you're an exception right now in this country. You've been married for twenty-five or thirty or forty years. How do you explain this? Why?" And the answer I got from those I spoke with was "I can always depend on my spouse to give me reflective backtalk."

Now, it struck me that this is really what leaders need. Not just from spouses, but from the people within their organizations and from the people without. One way that we continually grow as people, not just as leaders but as individuals, is through a lot of this reflective backtalk. And how do we create the architecture, how do we create the organizations and systems that would help us create incentives for that?

Townsend: I think there are two reasons for CEOs' maintaining long-term marriages. One is the effectiveness of the spouses. Many of the leaders might not have made it to CEO without their wives' (or husbands') help, encouragement, and flat-out management. Reflective backtalk is a small part of that. Remember, Bill Clinton, as a senior in college married to Hillary, was voted most likely to be president. Hillary was voted most likely to know what to do about it. Second, the spousal perks and rewards of a Fortune 500 CEOship must grease a lot of squeaky marriages. Check out the divorce rate among those who deserved the job but got passed over.

Getting back to your very important question about how to create a climate in which reflective backtalk flourishes, one of the methods that I used was to hire or promote only those I would like to work for myself. Good test. You can be wrong, because, as you know, in interviews people frequently fool you. But if that's the principal test, you tend to wind up with strong people. And I got wonderful reflective backtalk from my people; I remember one guy in particular who, when he absolutely disagreed with something I wanted, always started by writing, "Dear Jefe de Oro," which is what he called me. Translated it means "Chief of Gold," a sort of Inca-like form of address. "Dear Jefe de Oro: If you say so, it will be my hourly concern to make it so. But before I sally forth in service of this, your latest cause, I must tell you with deep affection and respect that you're full of it again. . . ." And then he'd tell me why I was wrong. His batting average was about .900 on those memos. And thank goodness for those memos, because he snatched me back from disaster several times.

Bennis: What you were also able to do was to encourage that dissent. You know, you were encouraging people to say, "Look, hey, stop." And one of the hardest things for leaders to do is to create a culture, an architecture that will enable that honesty to come forth—where it's no longer courageous to do it, it's just sort of matter-of-fact to do it.

And, you know, some leaders, realizing how powerful they might be, support dissension. Lee Iacocca's an example, but what Iacocca did—because he knows people are intimidated by the shimmer of his reputation, his charisma, and all that—is at all key staff meetings he appointed a devil's advocate or what he called a "contrarian.'' The contrarian takes the contrary point of view to whatever the group is going to decide on and confront, and is legitimized for it. It's a way of making sure the group's thinking isn't being steered in one direction.

Townsend: I like the idea of a rotating devil's advocate. There's another thing that I think a leader needs in this regard; at least I had it and it was terribly important to me. Donald A. Petrie, a partner at Lazard Frères investment bankers in New York City—a man I trusted implicitly and still do—gave the company 50 percent of his time. I was able to talk to him on the telephone and use him as a sounding board.

And frequently, you know, he pulled me back from the precipice and gave me the reasons why I was doing something I shouldn't do. I don't know how a chief executive operates without someone like that. Yes, I do. The answer is ''Not very well.''

Bennis: You were not just lucky. You cultivated that. If there's one thing that I would give as a tip to newly minted MBAs and others aspiring to a leadership position, it would be to get somebody in their lives on whom they can depend for that reflective backtalk that you were getting from Petrie. More than one is terrific, but you've got to have at least one.

Townsend: Mentors, would you call them? In the company or outside?

Bennis: Usually it would be outside, because I think it's real tough to have one inside. When you said ''mentor'' I was thinking I'd rather use the word *coach.* If I'm going to a coach to improve my form, I'm going to tell him the truth. You know, I've got to strengthen my form and my serve is lousy. It's very hard to reveal your weaknesses to your own boss. Whereas an "uncle" or "aunt" whom you don't report to directly would be a terrific person. And I think that's often the way it happens in institutions. It's usually some person a little bit outside the chain of command whom you can really relate to and who will be helpful. Maybe someone a little higher than you in the organization, a little older and wiser. One of the things I would do with my boss is to be clear about what I'm doing with my "aunt" or "uncle." And I think the boss would probably appreciate it. Because the more mentors or coaches you have, the better off you are. Now, I don't think your boss would be threatened, and I'd be very straight with him or her. . . .

Townsend: Especially if you consulted your boss on the selection of that mentor.

Bennis: That's a very good idea. Yes, very good. And he might also say, "Look, you can share with me. I'm open to this stuff. I mean I'd like to be your coach too," and that would be great.

I remember a marvelous panel that newsman John Chancellor moderated of all the past chiefs of staff to U.S. presidents. And the first question he asked them made me respect John Chancellor a great deal. By the way, he had them all there: Ham Jordan, who worked for Carter; Ted Sorensen, who was Kennedy's chief of staff; Bob Haldeman, who worked for Nixon; Andrew Goodpaster, who was Eisenhower's staff secretary; and Dick Cheney, who worked for Jerry Ford. The first question he asked was this: "Look, you've all worked for the most powerful man in the world. Certainly at one time or another he must have had a harebrained, damned fool idea that you knew would get him or the country into trouble. What did you do?" And he turned to Bob Haldeman on his right and he said, "Bob, let's start with you." And after Haldeman answered, Sorensen said, "Well, all *I* had to do was tell Mr. Kennedy that that was an idea Nixon would have had, and he would drop it immediately."

Townsend: That's great. Another way to encourage reflective backtalk is through the incentive compensation system. There was no cap on the incentive compensation system at Avis, and by the third year people were making more in bonuses than their base salary. Now you come up with a harebrained idea in a meeting and it isn't going to be some senior executive, it's going to be the regional vice-president for the northeast who says, "Hey, wait a minute. You're taking me and my company over the cliff." You're threatening his bonus.

Bennis: You see, that "Hey, wait a minute" also implies something about the self-esteem of the boss. People perceive that the boss can take it. I never thought of this before at all, but it's easy to confront certain bosses because you know that they're not going to be threatened by a difference of opinion. This has to do with self-knowledge again and having enough self-esteem. And people can smell it. They can smell when people are too fragile to take it or when they're too threatened to take it.

Townsend: We all have to build an artificial delay mechanism. Whenever our ideas are attacked, we have a genetic rush to defend them. A good leader will delay that impulse and ask for more attack. I think one of the defining differences between "good" positive self-regard and "bad" egocentricity is the capacity to encourage reflective backtalk.

Bennis: Another way of looking at it is this: The leaders I've observed don't try to prove themselves, but they do *express* themselves. I don't think they worry so much about what people think of them. They're able to take disapproval. They have enough sensitivity to really be able to listen to others. And that's a very difficult kind of path to take.

I hope this is clear, because I think it's terribly important. You cannot personalize the things you're going to hear, because you can't do a job as a leader if you're not going to overthrow the system, if you're not going to open things up, if you're not going to rock the boat—and then you have to handle the criticism that such measures invite. I mean, if there's one thing that's true of leaders today, it's that they have to change the system.

As Machiavelli once said, "Change has no constituency," and you're bound to get a lot of abuse. So, how do you develop the cuticle to take the abuse and still maintain sensitivity toward other people? I don't know how you can do that except by having enough positive self-regard.

Dialogue Starters

1. PARTNER ANALYSIS: **How well do you know yourself? List five strengths that you possess and have your partner tell you how well you demonstrate these strengths. Now switch and do the same for your partner. Next, determine three or more goals that would incorporate and develop these strengths. Work with your partner to determine whether or not they are realistic and in what time frame they could be accomplished.**

2. DEBATE QUESTION: What if someone in your organization were to come to you as a leader to "open things up and rock the boat"? One person takes the position that too much change can overwhelm a company unnecessarily and things need to be altered gradually. The other person takes the stand that without a total, top-to-bottom overhaul, things can stagnate and ultimately you will be damaged by the competition.

How do you become the best "you" possible, to be an effective leader?

Bennis: All of the leaders I talked with agreed that no one can teach you how to become yourself, to take charge, to express yourself, except you. But there are some things that others have done that are useful to think about in the process. I've organized them as The Four Lessons of Self-knowledge, and they are: (1) You are your own best teacher. (2) Accept responsibility; blame no one. (3) You can learn anything you want to learn. (4) True understanding comes from reflecting on your own experience.

First, you are your own best teacher. I want to put it very simply—learning is experienced as a personal transformation. A person doesn't gather learning as possessions, but rather becomes a new person. To learn is not to have; it is to *be*.

Next, accept responsibility; blame no one. I know this seems intuitively obvious—it does to me—but I'd like you to listen to one of the people I interviewed. Martin Kaplan, a very young leader at Walt Disney, is the best example of accepting responsibility for oneself that I know of. At thirty-seven, Disney Productions Vice-President Marty Kaplan has embarked on his third career. He came to Disney with a really interesting background—from biology to the *Harvard Lampoon,* from broadcast and print journalism to high-level politics. He knew a lot of different things, but very little about the movie business. In fact, he was a novice when he came to Disney. His description of his self-designed "university" illustrates how he accepted the responsibility for creating his own success.

He said, "Before starting this job, I put myself through a crash course, watching five or six movies every single day for six weeks. Then I read as many of the scripts as I could get my hands on to see what made these particular movies great. I kind of invented my own university so that I could get some sense of both the business and the art. I've always been in worlds where knowing the community has been important. In graduate school when I was studying literature, to know the writers and critics was to know a universe. In Washington, I had to know the political players. And here I had to learn the players. It became clear to me that there were about a hundred core screenwriters, and I systematically set out to read a screenplay or two by each of them.

"When I got here I was told it would take me three years to get grounded. But after nine months, the head of the studio told me I'd graduated and promoted me—by the way, that's Jeffrey Katzenberg—and told me my performance was on a par with my peers who had spent their entire careers here. One thing I did when I first got to Disney was to sit in the office of the studio head all day, day after day, and watch and listen to everything he said or did. So when writers would come, when producers would come, I would just be there. When he was making phone calls, I would sit and listen to him and I would hear him contend with what a person in his position contends with. How does he say no to someone? How does he say yes? How does he duck? How does he wheedle? How does he coax? I would have a yellow pad with me and all through my first months, any phrase I didn't understand, any piece of industry jargon, any name, any maneuver I didn't follow, any of the deal-making business, financial stuff I didn't understand, I'd write it down. And periodically, I would go trotting around to find anyone I could get to answer." That's Marty Kaplan's self-designed university.

Townsend: Maybe Marty Kaplan is sui generis. He certainly capitalized on an interesting opportunity. In any event, the first lesson, you are your own best teacher, is not in my repertoire. As a matter of fact, when Felix Rohatyn hired me from American Express to be CEO at Avis, I protested that I didn't know anything about the rent-a-car business. He said, "It's a people business. You're hired to run people. The minute you start sounding like an expert on the rent-a-car business, you're fired!" I'm amazed that anyone could learn the movie business in nine months. I spent two years at Twentieth Century–Fox as senior vice-president of international marketing and I'm sure I understood less about that business when I left than the day I walked in. I don't know if that statement is more revealing about me or Marty Kaplan or the feature film business.

Bennis: Third, you can learn anything you want. Keeping on my discussion with Marty Kaplan, I suggested that the kind of learning that he went through in his self-designed university had to do with reflecting on experience.

By the way, this is what you and I have been talking about quite a bit—biased toward action. Get up to bat as many times as you can. Practice as much as you can. *As-*

sume responsibility. Kaplan said, "I would have to add a component, which is the appetite to have experience. Because people can be experience-averse and, therefore, not learn." Unless you have the appetite to absorb new and potentially unsettling things, you just don't learn.

Townsend: I don't know how you assume responsibility if you don't have it. But I love the idea. If you can get away with it, it would be a great way to learn a lot of unsettling things.

Bennis: Finally, true understanding comes from reflecting on your experience. And reflecting on experience is a means of having a Socratic dialogue with yourself, asking the right questions at the right times in order to discover the truth of yourself and your life. What really happened, why did it happen, what did it do to me, what did it mean to me? I don't know how else we learn. I mean, maybe some people can learn from books alone. But I think there's just a profound difference between an academic who has read up on leadership and lectures about it, and a guy like you, Bob, who has experienced it.

Townsend: Well, Warren, you haven't exactly been a professor all of your life. You were president of the University of Cincinnati and, as I recall, that was about the time when the inmates took over the management of the institution. So you had real hands-on management experience, as well.

Bennis: I think it's true of every clinical area, whether we're talking about medicine, whether we're talking about writing, whether we're talking about lawyering, parenting, loving. I don't think there's any substitute for learning through experience. This is the life we learn with. You're not going to become a good surgeon by just looking. You've got to do it; you've got to have that experience. I think that's true of all those areas of life that are really important. And it's got certainly to do with leading.

Townsend: No argument with that.

Bennis: The journey of discovery has everything to do with reflecting upon your experience. Now you may need others to help you with that. That's why I think it's important to solicit advice and feedback and reflective backtalk from people you value. That's why I recommend to executives they keep journals. That's why I recommend to people that they take sabbaticals. Anything that will get you to take a look at yourself.

When I asked executives how they learned and why they had been forced to reflect upon experience, you know what they often told me? Many had suffered through an unhappy marriage and divorce. In another case I can think of right offhand, a daughter in the family committed suicide. It was amazing to me to see the extent to which personal hardships forced people to start, maybe for the first time, looking at their lives. Experiences like being fired, like having to fire people, like being demoted—these were the things people said they learned from.

Because, you see, these things scream out for explanation. Learning men and women try to understand it. The people who don't learn, I can promise you, are not going to get very far in life, let alone institutions.

Townsend: I think people who are going to become leaders have to make up their minds that they're going to have to change themselves. They're not going to get any help. They're obviously going to have to understand the major points that we're talking about and find out what they're comfortable with and then try it. From that they'll learn. Then they may be tempted to try something else that they didn't think they could ever do. But they're going to have to change themselves into leaders; there's no school for leaders.

Bennis: Yes, I think that's right. I think the way I would put it is, how do you manage yourself? That's what you're saying there. You can be perhaps prompted, there can be a trip wire, there could be a catalyst, but basically it's up to you. If would be great if there was a nice easy recipe or solution, and we could say, "Do this."

You know, that's why I sort of resent some of the books on leadership and management, which imply if you do the following things, you are guaranteed success. Like a fast-food metaphor of learning about leadership. You put a person into a microwave and out pops a McLeader? It just doesn't happen that way.

Leaders really invent themselves. They don't contrive— they really learn to put together a self, a person who is their own creation. Time and time again, I've seen that people who are great leaders seem to learn so much, and they keep learning from their experiences. There's a French word, *bricoleurs*—people who make pieces of art from, you know, bric-a-brac. They piece together an integrated person. They craft their lives. This is what I mean by self-invention.

Townsend: There's another meaning to *bricoleur.* It's an inventive handyman or tinkerer who can put together unrelated odds and ends and come up with a solution to a difficult problem. Claude Lévi-Strauss used this activity, *bricolage,* to differentiate human beings from apes until someone discovered that chimpanzees chew on stalks and then stuff them down antholes so the ants will rush out and the chimps can eat them. But *bricolage* definitely applies to a good leader, too. It explains how successes magically emerge in well-led companies from apparently hopeless situations. A leader does the best he can with what God gives him.

Dialogue Starters

1. DEFINITION EXERCISE: Define the characteristics you value in yourself as a leader and in a leader you admire. How many of the characteristics you listed for yourself are born from experience? Can you pinpoint what occurred in your life to create these characteristics?

2. WHAT-IF DISCUSSION: Discuss with a partner what would happen if you followed in the footsteps of Martin Kaplan and sat in the office of the person in the top leadership position of your company. What might you learn about leadership style that you never knew before? Might this give you more insight into this person's decision-making style, priorities, or frustrations? Perhaps this might be something you would actually consider doing at your company. Check it out.

Chapter 4

The Guiding Vision

Leaders are the most results-oriented people in the world, and this fixation with outcome is possible only if a person knows what he wants. Knowing what you want and being able to translate it into action are two more keys to effective leadership.

There are a number of ways a vision is developed, but most of our attention will be on getting your followers— and others—energized about making the vision an organizational reality. Vision grabs. Initially it grabs the leaders, and through their enthusiasm, followers and other stakeholders start paying attention. A company's attention is sustained, though, only by what the leader does and how he acts in pursuit of the dream.

Vision conveyed to the organization through action brings about a confidence on the part of the followers, a confidence that instills in them the belief that they're capable of doing whatever it takes to make the vision real.

On the other hand, a vision that can't be acted on because of cluttered company structure or useless rules is demoralizing, and sometimes destructive. When we discuss transforming *the organization, this is part of what we're talking about: cleaning up the system so it will embrace good leadership, not subvert it.*

—ROBERT TOWNSEND

What does it mean to have a vision?

Bennis: One of the most interesting leaders I've spoken with recently is from a major medical school and hospital. The organization has a budget of, I don't know, almost a billion dollars. It's a huge enterprise in New York. He said, "I spend most of my time reminding people of what's important." He had never administered anything other than a task force on gerontology. He got pushed up into this incredible job, people didn't even know whether he could start a car or tie his shoelaces, and here he's been put in this complex administrative role. I said, "What has been the most surprising thing to you?" And he said, "Well, in the first place, the number of stakeholders involved in the hospital. I just had to get to know the territory, to quote Harold Hill, the salesman in *The Music Man*. But I have to keep reminding people of what's important. Our job here," he said, "is to get patients to be better, to be well." And he said, "Everything else is a cost. Everything else is a commentary."

We can call it vision, we can call it strategic intent as they do in the management literature. Basically, it's a sense of knowing what the leader wants. There is a highly admired Romanian-born orchestra conductor, Sergiu Comissiona, who has conducted the Baltimore and Houston symphony orchestras and is considered one of the best young conductors in the world. When I asked members of the Aspen Music Festival orchestra why he was so terrific, I was surprised at their response because it seemed so simple. One after another said, "He doesn't waste our time." What kind of an answer is that? That doesn't sound so terrific. "He doesn't waste our time." But when you think about it, it means that he was always clear about his intention, his purpose, and what he wanted. Which didn't mean he couldn't change in the course of the rehearsal or the master class. As a matter of fact, I began watching him very closely at Aspen in his master classes and his rehearsals, and it was always extraordinarily clear and simple as to the kind of sound he wanted. And if there's one thing direct reports, followers, especially professionals, want to preserve, it is their time. What is more valuable? When you have a clear strategic intent, when you have a clear sense of purpose or point of view, I think it saves a lot of people's time. Again, I want to also insist on the fact that what transpired between him and the orchestra could change that point of view. It would shift over time, but it was always very clear.

When I think about the times in my own experience as a leader when I felt ineffective, it was almost always because I wasn't clear as to what I wanted from the particular sessions. What was the outcome? All the significant leaders I've ever met had the scorecard of results in their back pockets.

So, it takes strong strategic intent, purpose, vision, mission, objective, goal, I don't care what you call it. I use these words synonymously. Lots of people quibble—a lot of management theorists say, "What is the difference between mission and vision, goals, and strategic objective?" I'm talking about your capacity to communicate your intent, your purpose to others. And that's what Comissiona had, what I think all significant leaders have.

Townsend: The problem that I have is with the visionary watching his company drown in the swimming pool while he's searching the horizon for the next direction. It seems to me that we have to place vision in its proper time frame. It seems to me that the company has to achieve a certain amount of profitability, cohesion, concentration, and focus before vision can be communicated to everybody. Then the followers can use the vision to help them make decisions without having to consult with anybody, which is what you're trying to do with a vision, among other things. What we've done is say to companies, "You have to have a vision." What bad leaders have done is widely circulate a three-page statement of mission and values and emblazon it in Lucite in the lobby. It doesn't do anything.

Bennis: That's the Lucite plaque metaphor. But every great leader I've ever known and read about or personally interviewed is a pragmatic dreamer. I mean there's always vision, but there's an execution. Walter Wriston, former chairman of Citicorp, and I were talking about long-range plans and vision, and he said, "Look, for me a long-range plan is a dream with a deadline." So there are always both. I don't want to dismiss the vision thing because without it I don't think we have meaning or purpose or empowerment. But you're right, it isn't enough. Vision means nothing unless it's sustained in action. It's got to have a number of different action steps by leaders of the organization before it really makes any sense at all and before it can really be sustained in the organization. So every single announcement or pronouncement or edict always has to be sustained by organizational action. Without that, the words are empty and meaningless.

There's a company in downtown Los Angeles that has the most beautiful vision statement I've ever seen. It is called the Six Commitments. And this vision statement is decked out in every single office on a beautiful Lucite plaque. I'll tell you something, it is a brilliant vision statement. The Six Commitments are probably the hopes and aspirations of almost any good corporation or organization. The interesting thing about them is that not one of them is anchored in or corresponds with any organizational realities.

For example, one of the Six Commitments is "We honor the autonomy and integrity of our employees and believe in self-managed work groups." It takes six signatures to get permission to drive twenty-five miles out of downtown Los Angeles in this large utilities company.

I sometimes think that the zealous turn toward vision has been prompted by the Lucite companies that manufacture these gorgeous plaques, or these laminated cards that I see people pull out of their pockets. But what's interesting is, unless the vision is really anchored in reality, it can be destructive.

The second point I want to make is very close to what you are saying, that the very best leaders seem to embody and marry the visionary capacity with the management capacity to execute. Usually they're seen by many people as two separate types embodied in one person. The very best leaders have both.

Bill Walsh, the former coach of the San Francisco 49ers and of Stanford's football team, whom I've observed and interviewed, is a visionary—he really does think through every single defense maneuver available to the opposing team. He visualizes their major defenses. He calls the first twenty plays of a game based on his visualization. But he also cares about detail. He hired all the assistant coaches for the 49ers. He's desperately concerned about equipment and safety. You may recall the last eleven plays of the '89 Super Bowl where Joe Montana scored the winning touchdown against the Cincinnati Bengals. Walsh called all eleven of those plays within ninety seconds. When I was with him in the 49ers' locker room, I noticed he picked up papers, he straightened up pictures. Vision alone can not only be meaningless but can create cynicism and doubt. At worst, a vision combined with mixed messages can lead to organizational paralysis.

In one company I studied, the visions were coming down every month. They said they called it the vision-of-the-month company. And because they didn't know what was going to be expected of them, they stood still. They didn't know which way to go. So I think vision can be misleading. I even have a difficult time lecturing on it right now when I'm out giving talks on the qualities of leadership. I know it's important and it's got to be there, but without the capacity to deploy it throughout the whole organization, it can really be hurtful. As the Bible says, "Where there is no vision, the people perish." Without a point of view, where are you? Without vision, where's the meaning? It's one of those intricate, complex factors of leadership.

Townsend: I think what you're describing is vision that was written by the PR Department with the chief executive's help and cooperation . . .

Bennis: Yes.

Townsend: . . . and that is the wrong way to go at it.

Bennis: Exactly. I'll give you another beautiful example of that: Bob Haas, the head of Levi Strauss, had a vision statement prepared by his PR types—a beautiful statement. And he said, "Now what do we do? Take all of our twelve thousand people in the San Francisco area, march them to Candlestick Park, read them the vision statement, then go home?"

Dialogue Starters

1. MANAGEMENT EVALUATION: What is your vision for the company? How good is the management in communicating this vision? What actions does it take to ensure this vision is successful? Is the leadership able to successfully marry vision with execution? Brainstorm five techniques management could use to do this better.

2. GROUP DIALOGUE: Get together with four or five other people with whom you work and determine what aspects of your job might be a waste of time—what elements don't contribute to the overall vision of the company. Discuss ways to become more focused in accomplishing your company's goals.

How can a leader communicate his or her vision?

Townsend: In my experience, a leader has to be patient and has to talk to a whole lot of people, some of whom he may not like particularly, at a whole lot of levels of the company, and try to construct a vision out of conversations with them. What their convictions are . . . what we should do differently . . . what we should stop doing . . . what we should start doing . . . what we can do well and what we can't do well.

And out of that comes a statement of the vision that he can then take back and try out on everyone until finally everybody's light bulb goes on when he says the magic words. And I say that advisedly—it's *say* the magic words, not present them on a Lucite plaque. It has to be communicated verbally, or it won't work.

Bennis: Eyeball-to-eyeball.

Townsend: Yes, and then it's articulated by not only the leader but his entire cadre.

Bennis: But what puzzles me is, in a large organization, like Levi Strauss, for example, or your experience with Avis, or my working in the university, how do you meet with everybody personally?

Townsend: I think you have to start off with a rough goal, which is so simplistic that everybody will agree on it. In Avis's case it was "Let's try to get into the black." We'd never done it in thirteen years. It seemed like a fairly obvious thing. I mean, you don't have to talk to a whole lot of people to get agreement on that. You communicate that to everybody you meet, whenever you meet them. Then you start measuring your progress toward that, you feed the progress back, and you start rewarding the progress. Then you start decluttering the organization, i.e., getting rid of the excess baggage, which means all the work that isn't necessary as well as the people who do it.

And by that time, you have people very focused and control is not necessary, really. They're controlled by the reward system, by the clear goal, even though it's simplistic and short term, and by the fact that they're involved in it and they're being rewarded and they're getting frequent feedback. Work becomes fun—a new experience for many people. At that time, the leader's job becomes to go around and talk about the real vision. He takes six months to talk and listen to the top 10 percent of the company or the top five hundred people, plus random encounters: "What do we really want to become here? What do we have a good shot at doing the best at?"

At the end of six months, he's got a better vision. A vision instead of a simple, short-term goal. And he's also played that back to his team and to the next layer down and he has a general agreement. Then the team members—all of your department heads in your university, for example—are saying the same thing to the janitor and to everybody else: "This is what we're going to become." If the leader has done his six months' work well, he's got it right and he won't have to change it and send new memos around every month.

Bennis: Or those nice laminated cards. I think when we talk about how we make visions real, we have to get it so that people understand them, not just in their minds but in their hearts and in their guts. In addition to just interacting, for which there is no substitute, I was impressed with the ways several leaders I've observed went about communicating.

Robert Redford's first time out as a director was with the film *Ordinary People*, which later won several Academy Awards, including those for best picture and best director. Redford did a very interesting thing by way of making his vision real in working with cinematographers. There were all kinds of wise guys, who were very skeptical of this "too handsome, youngish debutant" director. To give them his idea of the way the film ought to look, he said, "I want you to indulge me by doing this exercise. I'm going to play some music for you and I'd like you to close your eyes while I play it, and to visualize the way this movie ought to open. Because I want it to open in an affluent suburb with the leaves just turning color and the kids returning in the fall to school. But I want you to close your eyes and think about what this scene, what the color, the tone, the texture of the film would look like if you listen to this music." So he had this hand-held cassette player and he put on Pachelbel's Canon in D, which starts off very slowly. Now, here are these very cynical guys who get caught up in this exercise but manage to come out with some very creative stuff. What he did was use an old trick called synesthesia, where you transform one sense into another. Walt Disney used synesthesia years ago in *Fantasia*. Redford also elicited his employees' participation so that he could make his vision real. But this technique was also, by the way, an interactive effort. The film is a testament to its effectiveness. Those are two examples that come to mind.

I remember when Frances Hesselbein took over the Girl Scouts. One of the first things she did was change the logo. She changed the pin. The Girl Scouts started in 1912. Because it was just before World War I, a warlike atmosphere was pervasive throughout the country. The Girl Scout pin, when she took over, conveyed this warlike feeling. It was an eagle with a big set of claws. It looked like a logo for the 10th Armored Division, not the Girl Scouts of the United States of America. She got a very good designer named Saul Bass to redesign the Girl Scout pin. While it sounds like a simple thing, it was the crucible for all kinds of changes that she intended that were very, very important symbolically. She got agreement. Getting that pin designed took the same finesse as what Redford did—he enrolled people in creating his vision, and so did she in getting this new pin designed by Saul Bass.

Dialogue Starters

1. DEBATE QUESTION: **Where do the ideas for a company vision originate? One partner takes the point of view that vision must grow from the members of a company and that the leader's role is to create a consensus based on the information given by his employees. The other partner takes the point of view that vision should originate from the top and then be communicated down through the ranks, since a leader probably knows what's best for the company.**

2. LISTING EXERCISE: **When was the last time you were really impressed by the way a leader communicated his or her vision? List five reasons why this person's communication technique was so effective. Now list five ways you feel a leader could spread his or her vision throughout a company, other than through the traditional Lucite plaque method.**

What impact does a leader's vision have on company performance?

Townsend: Back in the dawn of history, I was head of an investment department at American Express. We made our goal what we called the normal portfolio. We invested American Express's money, several billion dollars. But we had inherited a portfolio that was full of special situations, and many of them had losses. We wanted to maximize the return on this portfolio.

So simplistically we said, "This is what we've got, but let's make up a mythical portfolio that's more normal. We would like it to be based on what we know today, and then we'll just try to make changes toward that ideal over the years."

My role as leader was to support recommendations that might be vetoed at the top. The people at the top didn't understand; they didn't want to do this. I'd go in and eat a yard of carpet and back up the proposer and get the idea that had been proposed approved. And then we'd heave a sigh of relief because we were a little closer to our normal portfolio.

All of that, I think, is one role of the leader—to act out the belief of the company or act out his part in the achievement of the goal of the company. And if he's just playing golf with the top management and that doesn't get the job done, the people will start being nine-to-five time servers.

Bennis: I'll start with an example about high expectations. It comes from a very famous experiment done at Harvard roughly twenty-five years ago. It was a fascinating experiment, later referred to as the Pygmalion effect.

The experiment took fifty grade-school teachers in the Boston school system, and twenty-five were told that the students whom they were going to teach that semester were underachievers, and came from families that didn't care much about education. That was the set of expectations they gave the teachers. They told the other twenty-five teachers, "Look, the kids you got are terrific. They're high achievers. They come from families where they really value education."

Given that setup, it turned out that the scores of the kids whose teachers were told they couldn't learn actually dropped significantly by the end of the semester, by roughly twenty-five or thirty points. The scores of the kids whose teachers were told that they were going to be terrific achievers increased by about fifty points. In fact, the kids had been chosen at random. There was no difference between the two samples of kids. The only difference was what the teachers were told. When the teachers had high expectations, the students really performed.

I think the same lesson can be applied to management. I have never been disappointed by setting the highest expectations with my students, to the point where I say to them, "Look, if you can master this material in the next six weeks, you're going to know everything about this field that you need to know. You're going to be so well informed that you can say 'I don't know' and not feel insecure about it, but you're gonna work very hard in order to do that." That's what the Pygmalion effect is all about.

It's that sense of hope, that sense of optimism, that sense of "you can do it" that every winning coach can impart to his or her players, that every winning boss can impart to the work force, that every winning politician can impart to the nation. And I can't exaggerate the significance of creating those expectations as a real part of leadership.

There are a lot of ways of communicating the vision. When I say the more the merrier, it can go from videotapes to teleconferencing. And cartoons are marvelous because they take an abstraction and reduce it to a very common, concrete image. You know, Lyndon Johnson once said about one of his worst critics, Walter Lippmann, "Thank God he can't draw." Because the first thing that politicians turn to in the paper is not the editorial but the cartoon. Dr. Mitchell Rabkin, who runs a terrific hospital in Boston, Beth Israel Hospital, uses memos beautifully. His memos are pieces of poetry. They really do communicate. But sometimes it isn't the word that works, but the action.

I did a little personal survey of Beth Israel Hospital because I'm on the advisory board. I asked cab drivers, six of them in one weekend, "To what hospital would you take a patient who got ill in your cab? Or if you were in an accident, where would you go?" They all said Beth Israel. So the vision communicates throughout the whole community.

Rabkin spends countless hours going over the vision statement with his employees. The important thing is it has to be clear and demonstrated in action, not simply words alone.

Townsend: There are other actions you can take to let people know that you're open to feedback. You can ask them, "What should we stop doing?" as you go out into the field. And they'll say, "Why do we have to fill in this two-page report every month to the marketing department? I mean, *we* know who our market is. *They* know who our market is." Those are burdens that should be taken off the operating people, so that they can spend more time visiting their locations and solving problems on the spot. Those are things that are solid attention getters. It's one thing to go out in the field, which a lot of people don't do and should, but it's another thing to respond to the ideas that you get. Now you don't just go back to headquarters and write a papal bull. What you do is you go back and you sell what you've heard in the field to your cadre. And they don't all buy it the first time because nobody buys change. It involves effort.

So what happens is you wait a week and then you sell it again, using different words and coming at your people from a different angle, maybe with an example of what you were talking about on the table. And finally they all stand up and salute it. It becomes part of the operations of the company. When the people in the field are told they don't have to submit that monthly report anymore, they say, "Hey, there really is something new going on here!"

Dialogue Starters

1. BRAINSTORMING DIALOGUE: **What do people feel are the expectations from management in your company? Are they getting mixed messages? Brainstorm five new ways to communicate high expectations to others in the company. What can you do to reinforce positive results? Create an action plan that allows you both to communicate and to follow up on a vision of high achievement for others.**
2. GROUP DIALOGUE: **Do all the staffers understand how the vision in your company relates directly to them? Sometimes a vision is so broad that there is no link be-**

tween the big picture and the individual. Discuss ways that different areas of the department can translate the company vision into a mission that directly affects them. Now break down this definition even further to determine how a company vision affects each member of the company on an individual level. Share your answers with others.

Chapter 5

Creating a Trusting Organization

Trust binds leaders and followers together, and cannot be bought or mandated. It's also what sells products and keeps businesses humming. But what are the ingredients that create a trusting organization? Perhaps it's a charismatic leader, although there are certainly many trusting environments created by people who aren't necessarily charismatic. Maybe it's empathy, except even leaders who aren't empathetic can manage to build good working relationships. Certainly having a clear vision and focus is a part of it. But the best way to create a trusting atmosphere is to demonstrate trust in those you lead.

In this chapter, we'll discuss why you must trust others, how you earn your people's trust, and how to go about keeping it. You'll see why such ingredients as "the Four Cs"—congruity, consistency, caring, and competence—as well as good listening skills and the ability to promote understanding and empathy throughout an organization, are key to creating a trusting environment. The interaction between the leader and the led has been described as a "sweeping back and forth of energy." Through this process, unity is achieved—a team is built. The same transaction can occur for trust. *Ultimately, the way this energy sweeps back and forth is through constant, tireless communication.*

—WARREN BENNIS

How does a leader gain the trust of his or her people?

Townsend: A leader must be congruent. The old saw "I can't hear what you say because what you're doing speaks so loudly" is a perfect criticism of incongruity. It's why a leader can't be a phony. He can't pretend, he can't act, because it will become obvious almost instantly.

Bennis: And people are great detectives of phoniness, aren't they? It's amazing how we can spot it.

Townsend: You can't direct people to trust you. It starts with consistent action, trusting the people below you, even though they meet only 50 percent of your expectations for what you wish you had below you. You've got to convince yourself that they're capable of growing the other 50 percent. I mean really convince yourself. Because if you show a flicker of doubt, they'll pick it up immediately, spread it all over the organization by some magic communication system, and the energy will drain out. So you've got to start trusting down. And trust is earned by that. Eventually you'll be trusted if your actions are the same as your words.

You've seen many people, many executives, who exhibit no sense of trust at all. We don't have to speculate why. It could be because of the luxuries and a preoccupation with outside activities that they've lost touch with their organizations. But the main thing is, since they have no trust, they call in experts from the outside to give them reports on people. They hire handwriting experts; they hire outsiders and put them in over perfectly competent people. Hiring people from the outside demonstrates a lack of trust and maybe a lack of self-confidence.

Bennis: First of all, I think trust is the emotional glue of all institutions. You've got to remember that all institutions are human communities. Human communities, good ones, are based on a high degree of trust.

In your own experience, in your own life, what is it that generates and sustains trust? And I want you to think about a person whom you trust totally—what are the ingredients in that? What makes up that trusting relationship? Now think about a person you totally mistrust and why . . . aside from the fact that you can sometimes trust or mistrust a person immediately. Don't rely on that, because it's usually based on some old script in your mind about something that happened to you earlier on. As you said, Bob, trust is earned, it's interactive; there's no such thing as instant trust. Trust is composed of a number of ingredients including one we haven't talked about, but only implied, which is caring. Really caring about the fate of others, being on their side. I want to put that under the general category of the ways we generate and sustain trust in human institutions and in life in general.

One of the most interesting people I interviewed was

the movie director Sydney Pollack, who says one of the reasons he gets prima donnas like Barbra Streisand and Dustin Hoffman to work with him—and he gets them continually—is because they know he's got a track record of competence. They know he's put out a lot of movies that have won Academy Awards. Sheer competence is really important in generating trust.

I said earlier that most people think they have a good sense of humor and that they're honest. But that has nothing to do with congruity; trusted bosses, even if they're tough as nails, can generate trust because they're congruent individuals. That is, their goals match their inner feelings; they match what they say and do. This is what I think we both mean by congruity.

In the book that I coauthored with Burt Nanus, *Leaders: The Strategies for Taking Charge,* of the ninety leaders we mentioned, four of them were in *Fortune* magazine's list of the ten toughest and most difficult bosses in America. That included Jack Welch; John Johnson, who's the founder and head of *Ebony* magazine and insurance companies; and Andrew Grove of Intel. But what's interesting about all those people who were called tough is that they also were, in the cases that I knew about, highly trusted individuals because they were congruent. Their vision, their feelings, their words, and their actions went together.

Townsend: I've always regarded good listening as an exceedingly painful operation, because leadership is an eighty-hour-a-week job anyway, and most of the time you know what you're going to hear, or you *think* you know what you're going to hear, and you want to get it over with as soon as you can and get on to something else. And that's wrong.

You've got to listen patiently as if it's the most important thing in the world, because it is to the person who's talking to you and trying to persuade you to change your mind on something.

It's just essential, if the organization is going to be responsive, energetic, excited, and creative, to listen to all the problems. Then react the way you feel. You can say, "Listen, I've heard you and I know what you're saying, and I don't even know why I'm not going to do it, but I'm not going to do what you want," or "Come back to me later, right now it doesn't fit."

Bennis: What about the reverse? When you decide "Yes, hey, that's something I haven't thought of."

Townsend: It's a lot easier to be able to do that, to say, "I'm delighted, what a great idea, and I'm a dunce for not having thought of it." In most organizations people get the feeling that nobody is listening, nobody cares. And when you recognize and applaud a good idea it helps get rid of that perception in the organization.

Dialogue Starters

1. MANAGEMENT EVALUATION: **Assess the ability of people in leadership positions at your company to be congruent, consistent, caring, and competent. List any areas where they—or you—might fall short. Now assess the level of trust or commitment the employees of your company demonstrate. Do you see the connection between the Four Cs and the level of trust company-wide?**

2. GROUP DIALOGUE: **Discuss with your peers the elements that go into creating trust within a department. Do you agree with what Bennis and Townsend said or are**

there some factors they haven't considered here? Relate examples of ways you have been able to win over the trust of either a manager or someone you manage, being as specific as possible about the techniques you've used. Was there ever a time you lost the trust of someone with whom you work? What happened and what did you learn from the experience?

What are the most important aspects of being a good listener?

Bennis: I think two things are critical. If you really decide to listen, it has to have consequences, because it may mean you have to change. I think that having to change has something to do with being vulnerable because it may feel as if you're losing control, which is what every command-and-control-type leader gets anxious about. The other part is that the very act of serious listening itself, even if, as you said, Bob, you don't agree with it, is really so important. I think it's terrifically important because I've listened to people and, at times, I think that they've come away thinking, *Well, at least he understands me.* But I do think sometimes people don't even want to change—they really just want to be listened to and they want to be understood. That's the main thing. And it can't be phony; it can't be like putting on a smile and acting as if you understand. It's got to be a profound interest in what the person's telling you.

Townsend: I've got another way to promote understanding within an organization, Warren. When Avis finally broke into the black for the first time, our management developed a severe case of "us" versus "them"—"us" being the geniuses at headquarters and "them" being the people in the field in the red jackets who were renting cars and paying our salaries and doing an enormous amount of hard work. I sensed this from my travels and it worried me and I didn't know how to go about solving it.

Finally, at one Monday morning meeting, I said, "By the way, we're all going through the Avis school for rental agents at O'Hare Field." There were great screams of rage from these busy executive geniuses. I said, "Listen, it's not necessary. I'm not ordering you to do it. All I'm telling you is until you go through it with a passing grade, you're not in the incentive compensation plan." And to prove that I was serious, I said, "I'm going through it next week."

So we all went through it and it was a deadly course. We lived in a motel, we had a classroom, we attended class in the afternoon, we had a test every evening, we had homework to do at night, and all morning we were renting cars with trainee buttons on. One morning, I was renting a car at O'Hare and this customer came to the counter. I was taking a long time getting the keys right, processing the car control card, checking the credit card, smiling at the other people in line so they wouldn't drift over to our competitor. And he said, "Will you please hurry up? I'm in a hurry."

And I said, "Give me a break, I'm a trainee."

"Would you tell me how on earth a training program could pass somebody as clumsy and as ignorant as you seem to be?" he said.

And I said, "Well, if you want to hear something really sick, I'm the president of the company."

Whereupon he forgave me completely, and said, "Hey, at least you're out here figuring out what's going on. My president never leaves his office."

When we got through with that course, we were wearing red jackets at headquarters. The "us" and "them" thing was history. We were so proud of our people and what they were doing. We also realized that we were asking them to do an impossible job. And out of that came our first car rental computer, the Avis Wizard, which handled the rental agreement at the counter with the press of a button.

Bennis: If I can comment on what you just said, the symbolic value of that experience cannot be overestimated. The stories that went around the company as a result of that effort, the reverberations, the fact that all these top guys were really experiencing what employees were going through, must have been immense. Talk about empathic reach—doing it through action, not simply listening, has got to be the most effective method because I'm sure people thought about what others were going through. And that's what people want to know: Does management understand what we're doing before it puts out these vision statements or edicts?

Townsend: You can imagine the change in attitudes by management toward the "red jackets" whenever we went by a counter on a trip. You know, here was a heroine behind the counter, where before it was just some employee who was probably goofing up a rental agreement. Now it was someone who could do the job better than we ever could, and God help her and keep her.

The example that leaps to mind in protecting your people, another role of the servant leader, occurred very early in my career at Avis when I attended my first board meeting at Lazard Frères and Company, which owned Avis. On our board were all of legendary senior partner André Meyer's close friends, including David Sarnoff—General Sarnoff, the CEO of RCA. And the general did what all important people do at their first board meeting: He tried to impress other people with his intelligence. He said, "Mr. Townsend, I'd like to have a computer printout of all our vehicles by make, model, and location." And, you know, ninety-nine out of a hundred CEOs attending their first board meeting in the presence of the great General Sarnoff would have said, "Yes, sir. Right away. I will take over our entire accounting department and all our operations and in a month we'll churn this out manually for you." Which is what it would have taken.

Instead, I was motivated by fear, in large measure because one of Lazard's great moves was to insist I liquidate my small nest egg of stocks and bonds and invest everything in its leveraged buyout of Avis. It was a requirement, and it gave me a "take no prisoners" attitude toward any action that seemed to hamper the company's progress. And so fear gave me courage.

I said to the general, "With all due respect, General, if I don't need that statement to run the company, I don't know why you need it to be an outside director of the company." Whereupon he turned the color of a tomato. And he sputtered, but he didn't get the statement. Word got back to our accounting people and our operating people that I had saved them a month of stupid work.

And people changed their minds about management. *There's something new here,* they thought. *We've got somebody unusual, and maybe this is worth another try.* These people had been through several leaders and never made a profit and they'd felt like losers. At least their heads came up a little to see if there was anything new. I had gotten their attention and earned their trust.

But, mind you, when you start earning people's trust, you can't just do a little of it on Monday, and then betray them Tuesday, Wednesday, Thursday, and then do a little on Friday just before the weekend, and expect to get trusted back.

You have to earn their trust consistently. That's why you have to know yourself and know what you can do and be faithful to yourself. Be consistent and honor the trust that you've earned.

Bennis: Especially in today's fast-changing environment in which it's very difficult to generate that trust. The example I want to give you is American Medical International, Inc., after the Bass brothers bought 5 percent. Its chairman and its CEO assured the work force that AMI was not for sale. And their people believed it. When the Bass brothers bought another 5 percent, the employees read about it in the papers. And the company said again, we're not intending to sell. Fractional pieces of that company were bought out, against the wishes of the CEO and chairman of the board. What does that do for trust? In this case AMI's leadership was telling the truth, but still, later on, the company was, well, sold.

Townsend: Well, I can add something to that. . . . It doesn't put me in the greatest light. As I mentioned before, Avis was owned by Lazard Frères and Company when I was there. It owned 51 percent of the company. Anyway, one time Lazard Frères brought me into André Meyer's office to meet the CEO of Mobil. I was told the day of the meeting that I was going down there to meet a potential owner. We were then growing at 35 percent annually in our profits and were one of the most talked-about growth stocks. In an effort to fight off being acquired by a two-hundred-foot sponge and the extinction of our company—which is the way I looked at it—I said to the CEO of Mobil, "Why don't we wait about four years, and we'll buy you?" It was a preposterous thing to say, but it made it very clear that he wouldn't want me as an employee, and the acquisition was called off. After that I said to André, "I do not want to be a part of any discussions you have with potential buyers of this company. I want to be able to honestly say to my people, I don't know of any discussions. Now you go ahead and sell the company, but tell me about it after you've done it, with the understanding that I don't go along with the sale."

Bennis: One broad way of thinking about trust is to think about predictability. Good, effective teams are all based on trust; knowing that even on a bad day, I'm going to have someone who can compensate for that bad day. It's said about professional pitchers that, even on their bad days, they can win. And they win because they have a team backing them up that they can rely on. Watch the way football receivers do especially well with a passer they really trust and vice versa. It's that kind of thing that goes into what we're calling trust.

Dialogue Starters

1. BRAINSTORMING DIALOGUE: **Does every level of your company understand what every other level is doing? Do they support or relate to their peers and their problems? Brainstorm five techniques for promoting understanding and empathy throughout your organization. Now see what it would take to implement some of these ideas.**

2. DEFINITION EXERCISE: What is your definition of consistent leadership? Does it include the word *predictability*? Does it include the word *integrity*? How do these qualities relate to the notion of knowing oneself? How do these qualities affect the level of trust in a company overall? Envision some of your role models for leadership—define the characteristics they possess that suggest to others that they will consistently support their staffs.

Chapter 6

Empowerment

Good leaders and good followers share many of the same traits. In fact, the single most important characteristic of a follower may be a willingness to speak out and tell the truth, which is precisely the kind of initiative that makes good leadership. And when a leader creates an atmosphere in which employees feel free to offer contrary views and speak the truth, an empowered work force is created. Given the power to do what they do best, these motivated individuals serve as vital allies in transforming the organization.

A leader is rewarded for his or her efforts to create a workplace based on empowerment. When people feel significant, they're reminded by example that learning and competence matter, they feel they are part of a community effort, and, finally, they find their work challenging and stimulating. Giving your people the license to tell the truth means that you have to be prepared for criticism. It also means that, as Warren Bennis illustrates, you have to expect your people to admit their mistakes and ask for help in dealing with errors in judgment.

—ROBERT TOWNSEND

How can a leader empower his or her people?

Townsend: A leader can empower people by expecting more of them than they think they can possibly achieve. It's a self-fulfilling prophecy—if the leader really believes that people can do more, they'll begin to expect more from themselves. People can do incredible things and accomplish unbelievable tasks if their leader expects them to, and says so and communicates it by her behavior, not just by words or memos.

Bennis: I think empowering people is not only something that a leader should or might do; it's a duty, responsibility, and obligation of leaders to coach people to bring out their potential, to really be people growers.

Townsend: When a leader walks past the mail room and says, "Hey, Charlie, how are things going?" he doesn't keep on going before he gets the answer. He really looks at Charlie, and he really wants to hear how Charlie's doing. He doesn't send Charlie a memo saying, "I want you to be more aggressive and energetic and come in a little earlier and leave a little later and put a little more oomph into your job." That's not leadership. He asks Charlie how he's doing, and then listens carefully to the answer.

I got a newsletter from Tom Peters. There's a pop quiz in it that the Donnelly Corporation, which is one of the great companies that I visited twenty-two years ago in Holland, Michigan, asks its employees. It makes rearview mirrors for all the automobile companies. You can imagine how competitive that work is. And Donnelly believes in company surveys. If I'd had this when I was at Avis, I'd have been asking these questions as I went around the country talking to our people.

It's very hard for people not to answer these questions. First ask them, "What made you mad today?" That's a great question. It leads to two things: First, it reveals what's wrong with the organization, and second, it tells the person you've asked that you're interested.

Next ask evaluative questions such as "What took too long?" "What was the cause of any complaints today?" "What was misunderstood today?" "What costs too much?" "What was wasted?" "What was too complicated?" "What's just plain silly?" "What job took too many people, and what job involved too many actions?"

Now, you don't have to ask all those questions like that. But you can try one on one person, pass by another office, and try one on another person. What you're doing is telling people you're interested in how they feel about their work. That's part of leadership.

They feel important as a result. You don't send a memo saying, "You're very important, thank you very much."
Bennis: I think, more specifically, one thing leaders cannot help doing is being role models, whether they like it or not. We're all teaching leadership every single day we're interacting with our followers and with the people that we report to. We're really modeling, demonstrating what other people are going to copy. The way people learn in organizations, for the most part, is through observation.

They look to see definitions of success, and they look to see people who embody those things that can mean you get ahead or you don't. I think that people use their eyeballs and eardrums most of all. Albert Schweitzer, the great humanitarian, was once asked if he had any advice for parents about bringing up children. He said, "I only have three principles, three basic rules. One, you only teach by example. Two, by example. Three, by example." So whether you like it or not, you're in the business of growing or stunting the growth of leadership.

I like the model of a coach. One thing that interests me about coaching is that when you go to a coach, you don't try to deny or defend too much. You really talk about what your weaknesses are, because you're going there to get better. But I think there are two things you can do, three things maybe, and I want to say something about what you just said about setting high expectations. Give your people the license to tell the truth, remind people of what's important, and then set expectations of excellence. Again, I think you do this by modeling.

Very good leaders have that sense of elevating the possibilities of their individuals, and this is what growth is all about. Such things as optimism and hope can be learned. When you've had enough successful experiences working with a boss who cares about growth, you can learn optimism and hope.

I was talking about optimism and hope on a panel two years ago, and on the panel with me was a man named Richard Wirthlin. Maybe he's not a household name, but Wirthlin runs a polling survey company, and for seven years he was President Reagan's pollster. He said, "I want to tell you, Reagan is a beautiful example of what you're talking about. Back in the summer of '82, we hadn't gotten out of the recession yet, and his approval rating was thirty-two percent, which was the lowest of any president in the second year of office since polls were taken.

"At the end of March of '81, when there was an assassination attempt on his life, the day or two after, his polls, his approval rating had gone up to about eighty-five percent—the highest ever for a person in office the first year. So I said, 'Well, Mr. President, your approval rating is down to thirty-two percent which is about as low as it gets.' He said, 'What do you mean as low as it gets?' And I said, 'Well, it's the lowest since we've been doing polls on presidents for their approval.' He said, 'Oh' . . . and began smiling. Then he said, 'Dick, for God's sake, stop worrying, or I'll just go out there and try to get shot again.' "

Now I know that's a joke and all that, but I think there's something to this sense of hope and optimism, of setting high expectations, and at a national level that's what Reagan was able to do. What most people remember about Jimmy Carter is his famous malaise speech. The speech was rather interesting since he was talking about the energy crisis. But it did him in because it was about despair, which is the opposite of hope. Despair means no choice, no options. Hope always provides options, always provides some glimmer of "Yes, we can do it." That's what leaders have to communicate and embody and express in action.

Townsend: Optimism is related to a very important item that never gets mentioned enough: having fun in an organization. There's no reason why work shouldn't be fun. It almost never is, but that's the fault of the leader, in my opinion. Life is too short to get too serious about work.

And there should be down time and time to laugh about failure and mistakes.

I remember once back in my American Express Investment Department days, one of the guys who worked with me said after a particularly harrowing incident, "You know, Townsend, the funny thing about you is that the worse the crisis, the bigger your smile. I don't understand that." And I said, "I don't understand it either, but maybe it's just that it all seems pretty funny to me." We take each setback, each adverse development, so seriously. As Arthur Balfour, prime minister of Great Britain from 1902 to 1905, once said, "Nothing matters very much, and very few things matter at all."

You shouldn't discuss your plan with anybody else except your mentor, if you have one. You shouldn't discuss it with your boss, you shouldn't discuss it with the people who work for you, you should just think through what you've heard or read and make a plan that fits your personality for a different behavior, a different way of working, and a different way of dealing with your people.

For instance, you can turn your people loose. When someone comes into your office and says, "We've never been able to do this project or report or whatever, and it's ridiculous that we can't do it," you can say, "Why don't you try, and if whatever you're doing goes wrong, I'll take the flak, and if it goes right, you get the credit. But keep me posted so I know when I'm about to get shot in the back." And that person will go off and try something and maybe fail, maybe succeed, but the whole organization will suddenly begin to look up at you and see what's next and try things. And sure, you're running a little risk. I said "a little risk" because nobody likes change and nobody likes mavericks, and you could get some flak from upstairs.

But just weather the storm, roll with the punches, protect your people, and enjoy what you're doing, and pretty soon your organization will be having so much fun and will be so excited that its performance will be outstanding.

Bennis: The first lecture I gave to business people was when I began teaching at the Sloan School. My mentor, Doug McGregor, one of the great leaders in what's now called the humanistic area of management and management theory, was at my first lecture. These were Sloan Fellows who were in their mid-thirties. I was in my early thirties at the time, and I gave a lecture that was absolutely a bomb. There is no other word for it. I was totally unconnected and it was a disaster. Doug and I rode up in the elevator together, and he didn't say a word and I didn't say a word. I looked at him and, as we got to his office, I said, "Pretty bad, wasn't it?" He said, "Yes, let's talk about it." And we talked about it, but there was no punitive reaction. He just showed a tremendous amount of empathy for me and what I was going through.

You can imagine what it was like to fail that abysmally in front of my boss, for whom I wanted to perform at my best and show off. His response was so remarkable because he didn't deny my failure at all. He sort of chuckled a little bit. He didn't make light of my actions, he didn't make fun of me, but it was the incredible understanding he provided that I will never forget and that I will always try to model.

Townsend: What he did was encourage you to admit your mistake or your failure . . .

Bennis: Yes.

Townsend: . . . by smiling at you and saying, "Let's talk about it."

Dialogue Starters

1. WHAT-IF DISCUSSION: What if you gave those whom you lead the power to try to succeed or fail? What if *you* were given the power to try and succeed or fail? If that already happens in your organization, does it serve to empower people or scare them? What if you or your people did fail—would it ruin the company? Would it motivate others to try harder?

2. GROUP DIALOGUE: What are the techniques, if any, you currently use to empower your employees? Pretend it was up to you to change totally the way employees were empowered. Would you (a) create high expectations; (b) provide optimism and hope; (c) teach by example; (d) ask open-ended questions one-on-one; or (e) turn them loose and have fun? Discuss why each technique would or would not be effective.

How do you delegate responsibility to your employees?

Townsend: Let me give you an example. Here's this leader who's been a success in the organization, so she keeps getting more work dumped on her by a satisfied management. She just got another thirty employees dumped on her because her business has grown from $30 million to $100 million and they want to do in-house promotion instead of buying it outside. That's thirty new employees. She's already got no home life, and she's worried about burnout.

What does she do? We're talking about delegation, but it's also a question of leadership.

What she does is tell the rest of her organization to get along without her for ninety days and she goes over and runs the new thirty-person shop for ninety days. With her talents and experience she'll easily recognize the leader of that group, she'll know whom she can trust, and she'll know the whole business pretty well. Then, when the ninety days are up, she'll say, "Craig, you're the new leader of this organization. You report to me; I'm going back to do my regular job."

She then no longer needs to drown herself in activity and work an eighty-hour week. That's a form of delegation. She's not delegating to thirty people she doesn't know; that's very dangerous and it's stupid. She's not delegating a business she doesn't understand. She's taking the time and the risk of learning a new business, finding a relationship with a new person she trusts, and then going back and working a normal number of weekly hours. That's the way to delegate intelligently.

Bennis: I want to reframe the issue of delegation. The word sounds strangely quaint and rustic to me. *Delegate* sounds like I'm going to give a job to somebody else, who's working for me, to do. When you think about management today, you think about a team of people. You think about a boss or leader and a group. Delegating gets to be more complicated.

The way I used to run things, and I think the way very effective leaders do, too, is the following. List a set of functions that the organization or group needs to get done. What are the group's primary tasks? List also what people feel they want to do. And third, list what they're competent doing. Now, if you can get the right mixture of what needs to be done, what people want to do, and what they're competent to do, I think you'll have a high-performing, fully empowered team. That reframes the whole issue of delegation, because it's basically a team effort and not just the boss handing off the work, like a quarterback handing off the ball to a running back. That kind of delegation is not simple. But I do think we're going to have to enlarge the concept of delegation to a team effort that the leader can encourage.

A good example of this method is Pacific Bell and the problem it had in 1984. The company assigned two groups of people to set up—under unregulated marketing conditions—phone systems and communication systems for two events happening in California. Those events were the Democratic National Convention and the Olympics that were being held in Los Angeles.

These were presumably going to be temporary teams, and Pacific Bell brought them together from all parts of the company. The teams were terrific. They had to meet customer demands, they had to make money, they had to have fun—and they did. The problem was, how do you get those temporary teams back into Pacific Bell, to enliven and inspire that culture in the way that the teams were able to do? Separately, these people were leading dull, humdrum lives for Pacific Bell. But suddenly these same people were given this opportunity to have their own teams, they had to make money, and they did so beautifully.

Townsend: And the teams had a deadline, which is important, isn't it? What Pacific Bell did was create a crisis . . . and people have more fun in crises because there's going to be an outcome and you're going to win or lose. The teams wanted to win, and if they had to work eighty hours a week to win, they did. Besides, these people found out that they enjoyed the work.

I have a strong feeling against putting your colleagues into competing positions. "The survival of the fittest" is what it's called. I don't believe in that. I think you have to build an environment in which people cooperate with each other, help each other as much as they can. I once made the mistake of announcing a successor a year in advance of my departure. The rest of the employees tore him to shreds that year—the rest of the candidates who thought they deserved the job. He was gone before the time when he was supposed to take the job. I just don't believe in encouraging competitive energies within the organization among individuals.

I feel a little bit differently about teams. I think a certain amount of competition between teams can be healthy. But you have to judge, "Is this going to be destructive or constructive?" and do what's right.

Bennis: I think encouraging openness is important. There is a company I have worked with that provides an interesting case and it'll flesh out what you were just talking about. One of its mottos has to do with teamwork. That's value one. Value two is, you never express disagreement. Now think about that. How can you have a team that's really creative and hardworking without ever expressing disagreement? It means a very distant kind of team. You've got to express disagreement; you've got to deal with conflict; you've got to surface people's assumptions and deal with them.

Teamwork can get destructive, and that's where leadership is really important—to create balance. You cannot have a team without differences, and it's being able to treasure and work within the differences and still respect one another that really makes for effective teamwork.

Within a team, I think expressing dissent, expressing conflict, while keeping within a creative healthy range is very, very productive.

Dialogue Starters

1. GROUP DIALOGUE: A manager in your company has come up with a revolutionary new approach for increasing profits and is given the opportunity to organize her people in a manner that will make them the most efficient and productive. The catch is that her people have little expertise in the responsibilities they will be given. Discuss the advantages and pitfalls of the manager's delegating responsibilities to her people. Now discuss the advantages and pitfalls of having her create a team approach.

2. LISTING EXERCISE: Do employees feel free in your organization to express disagreement? List three different ways someone can constructively disagree and be heard in your organization. If you can't think of three ways, you probably need to reassess your organization. Do employees feel free in your organization to make mistakes? How much freedom are they given to do so? List three ways you can empower employees to feel freer to express their ideas and act on them.

Can you give an example of a company that functions solely through teamwork?

Townsend: W. L. Gore and Associates is a strange example of a company using teamwork. One of the strangest things about it is that nobody else that I know of has ever followed Gore's example. It's been in business for about thirty years now. It's up to five thousand associates, with forty-three plants in nine countries including the United States. It has no hierarchy, no vice-presidents, no managers, and it operates on the basis of a goal that everybody agrees to. Someone from the organization told me, "What we want to do here is make money and enjoy doing it. We have some minimal restraints. One is we must all agree to try to be fair: fair to our associates, fair to our suppliers, fair to our customers. We also agree that commitments are sacred. If I commit to another associate to help him with his project, he can count on it, he can take that to the bank. I cannot welsh on a commitment." In a structure without orders from vice-presidents or managers, of which there are none, the company operates on a self-commitment basis.

The company operates on these principles: It will try things and fail, and its employees will not have to go to anybody to get permission to try new things if they can answer yes and yes to the following questions. The first question is "If it works, will it be worthwhile to Gore?" And the second question is "If it fails in the most dramatic way, will Gore survive?" If an employee can answer yes to both those questions, that person can go ahead without permission from anyone. Those are the minimal restraints under which people operate.

As a result of getting from the goal to the vision, there are so many products in the four divisions that they don't even bother to count them anymore. All a person has to do is have a vision of a product that will make money and that he will have fun creating, a vision that is so attractive that he can recruit other associates to work on it with him. Or if he can't, he can work on the project alone. The essence of the Gore operation goes back to Bill Gore's experience at du Pont, where he had a long and happy career as a scientist, but he noticed a difference when he was between projects.

When he was working on the Teflon project, the people there worked crazy hours, they were excited, they could hardly wait to wake up in the morning and come to work. After the project was over, when he went back to his nine-to-five job, he couldn't account for the difference—how little energy he had, how little interest he had. So the whole Gore operation has been structured to retain that project energy and creativity. There are visions going off in all directions in the Gore organization. It's unusual, but it's a model that we should all reflect on when we're trying to build that kind of energy and creativity and excitement in an ordinary company.

A good organization, not built on the Gore principles, works sort of the same way. After they understand the reward system, the goal they're working toward, people get excited, they're energetic, they're enthusiastic, creative, they're solving their own problems—and there's no time for politics, no time for backstabbing, no time for regularly scheduled meetings. They just get on with the job. And they see the results in the monthly statements.

Bennis: What you and I are talking about is that the leader has responsibility for helping to create a culture that facilitates the growth of the individuals in it. Because if we think about any organization as being a human community based on trust, based on openness of expression, based on growth, the leader has to become the social architect of that culture and has great responsibility for facilitating the kind of climate that would foster and enable these things to happen.

They're not going to happen naturally, you know? They're going to have to happen by the interventions of leadership to model and to reward the expression of these things we're talking about.

Townsend: I don't think you write the culture statement in advance. What you do is work on the people to do what we talked about earlier, which is a trial-and-error operation most of the time, and in some way get them all coming to work excited, enthusiastic, and unafraid of making mistakes. If you do that, the rest will all come and the culture will emerge as whatever the culture is. Then you can have a go at writing down the culture statement and describing the culture, but not before.

Dialogue Starters

1. PARTNER ANALYSIS: Assess the level of enthusiasm and energy your department has for the work it does. Have your partner evaluate how you contribute to creating this type of environment. Now do the same for your partner. Together try to brainstorm ways to generate more excitement from your peers or the people you manage. Try to include the word *empowerment* in your answer.

2. DEBATE QUESTION: To what extent are leaders ac-

countable for helping to grow their people? One partner takes the position that a leader's job is to lead and delegate in order to ensure the department runs smoothly. Every person is responsible for his own growth. The other partner supports the belief that leaders must run the department through their people, and that requires a personal investment in their development on the job. Which type of leader would you prefer to work for? Which type of leader would you prefer to emulate? Are they the same?

3. MANAGEMENT EVAULATION: Have you ever worked for a boss and had the feeling "Hey, he really wants me to succeed"? Can you visualize yourself being such a boss? How might this affect your level of performance?

Chapter 7

Leading the Transformation

Up to now, you've learned about giving attention—to your own growth, to the growth of your employees and peers, and to the vision that you're striving to make real. This chapter focuses on getting attention and making changes in the organization. The business world is now more frenetic and more complex than at any previous time. This chapter will teach you how a leader can start transforming his or her organization so it can weather these storms and increase the quality of life for all involved. One way to do this is to shake things up. Leaders who risk making changes and moving away from the conventional standards of business practices often find themselves forcing the world to adapt to them, instead of having to adapt to the world.

Another way to make changes is to move away from the tried-and-true paradigm of COP, or control, order, *and* predict, *and incorporate a newer, better model called*

ACE: acknowledge, create, and empower.[1] In this chapter we'll explore what these paradigms mean and why it's important for leaders to unlearn behaviors in the past that have helped them get to their present levels of success. We also explore the notion of crisis and its advantages and how one can empower oneself by instilling an atmosphere of fun, friendliness, and flexibility in an organization.

—WARREN BENNIS

What are the characteristics of terrific organizations?

Bennis: In no particular order of importance, they go like this:

- Creativity; that is, rewarding creative, innovative behavior
- Long-term focus
- Cooperative/interdependent/collaborative behavior
- Risk taking
- Great concern for results
- High preference to assume responsibility
- High tolerance for ambiguity
- Openness to change
- High task orientation
- Primary focus on effectiveness, not just being efficient
- High organizational identification and pride
- A lot of mentoring and support for growing leaders
- Reducing distinctions in rank

1. Thanks to Roger Evered and Jim Selman for this formulation.

Throughout our conversations, we've talked on and off about a lot of these items. But I'm trying to condense an awful lot into these items I've just ticked off. Before we talk about how we change institutions, how we transform them, we have to decide: *to what?* We found these characteristics to be absolutely crucial in looking at those institutions that will be competitive in the year 2000.

A lot of organizations are stuck and are going to face crises if they already haven't. A new leader has to be able to change an organization that is dreamless, soulless, and visionless. Take ITT under Harold Geneen, for example; his goal was to increase earnings per share each quarter, period. That's what I mean by soulless and dreamless.

If we're talking generically about leaders coming into an organization like that, or even a smaller one, the first thing they've got to do is blow a whistle, kick the machine, do something that's going to indicate this is an entirely new day. Frank Dale of the *Los Angeles Herald-Examiner*—which was on strike for ten years, bottom line oriented, and a Hearst Corporation paper—settled the strike with the union and opened the front doors, which had been barricaded for eight years. Someone's got to make a wake-up call.

Townsend: One of the myths in organization and leadership is that it takes a long time to transform an organization. I thoroughly disagree with part of that. Certainly it would take a long time to change General Motors. Big organizations are very difficult to change. My point is, smaller organizations like Brunswick, the bowling and fishing equipment manufacturer that underwent a turnaround, can be and must be changed very rapidly or they won't change at all. You've got to get the attention of the people and make the changes while they're looking. The way you attack big organizations, if *attack* isn't too hostile a word, is you take the part of the organization that seems ready, then you make changes very fast. It's best if the CEO makes the changes himself. But if not, the changes should be done by somebody with conviction and urgency, and all the characteristics that we're talking about. Then you relax and wait for the feedback to go around the organization and benefit the people who have all become heroes in the organization. When that happens you begin to hear from other parts of the company that want to get on the list to do the same thing. Then you do it again. But each foray into change is done very rapidly.

Bennis: What I'm getting at is every single leader who wants to change an organization has to really make some very specific moves and actions early on. The first step, and I'm talking generically, is that he or she has got to do something that's dramatic, that's visible, and that has resonance throughout the whole organization—something that signifies direction.

Townsend: At Avis, what we did to hit the mule between the eyes and get its attention was set the goal. We had to get into the black, very simply. The goal later became: We want to become the fastest-growing company in the business of renting and leasing vehicles without drivers.

So here's this sleepy organization that never made a profit. What did we do? I got 15 percent of pretax profit from the owners for an incentive compensation system for the top people, and I defined the top people as the top one thousand people in the company. And they agreed to that readily because 15 percent of zero is zero and that's what I was asking for. The company had never made a profit. Then we went to enormous expense to construct one thousand profit-and-loss statements with somebody's name at the top of each one. Every location had a P&L of its own, with overhead laid back and allocated to that. Well, that's an enormous accounting effort, but we did it.

Meanwhile, we reformed the bank agreement and we reformed the car-purchasing agreements. We got the newest fleet; we got new uniforms; we got new logos and a new look. Then we just started going around the country and talking to people and asking, "What are we doing wrong? Why haven't we made any money in thirteen years? How can we survive without making any money?" And the ideas in the field from the people who were doing the work were exciting. Out of those trips to the field came the second vision.

Then the top two people, Donald A. Petrie, chairman of the executive committee, and I, exempted ourselves from participating in the first million of profits because we wanted the rest of the people to taste blood as soon as possible. The whole 15 percent of the profits went into the pay for the rest of the employees, about a thousand people in all. They began to get bonus checks and eyes popped open. The energy was focused and they all suddenly knew how to run a rent-a-car company. One of the problems was if you're operating in Tulsa, you've got four agencies and three locations, so you have to visit seven places a week, and they just hadn't been doing that. So now they started. "The first thing you have to do," we told them, "is visit your troops, see how they are, what the problems are, what the competition is doing that you're not doing. You've got the newest fleet in the industry. What are your excuses?" And after they began focusing, the company turned

around in no time at all. It was an exciting development.
Bennis: So one of the key issues you were just talking about
was, how do you focus attention? How do you get people's
attention? And when you look at theories of organizational
change, theories of transformation, they always have three
phases. One is the unfreezing phase, where you have the
wake-up call. The second is where you undergo a lot of
rapid change. And the third is kind of refreezing; you
know, installing the changes, making sure they're endur-
ing. This process is ongoing, it's three acts, but there's
never a completion of the third act. You've just got to keep
rolling over and continuing again.

But you also have to get your employees' attention,
make progress, measure progress, and see that your people
who are achieving the progress are rewarded for it. You've
got to keep them in touch with your vision.

Dialogue Starters

1. MANAGEMENT EVALUATION: Assess the efficiency and effectiveness level of your organization. What is your
greatest problem area? When was the last time someone
made an effort to shake things up there? Discuss whether
or not this approach is the surest way to progress. List the
specific steps you might take to effect change.
2. DEBATE QUESTION: When is it necessary to transform an
organization? Every few years? Only when things aren't going well? When new leadership is introduced? Debate the
positive and negative aspects of making changes during
each of these periods. What influence does timing have on
effecting change?

What paradigm are companies presently operating under?

Bennis: Right now, all American institutions, and probably institutions worldwide, are between two paradigms. One paradigm is best illustrated by Bob's caricature of that tough leader of the nineteenth century who worked pretty well in a bureaucratic structure. The paradigm for that structure is best described in three words: *control, order,* and *predict.* That kind of structure isn't going to work in today's environment. When I say we're between two paradigms, the other paradigm is still formless, still not clearly articulated, but if I could assign three words to this unknown paradigm, they would be: *acknowledge, create,* and *empower.* We're talking about network organizations. Most organizations, while they may aspire to the new paradigm of acknowledge, create, and empower, are still stuck. I've talked to experts and made lots of observations about where most organizations are. Though many espouse the new empowered organization, which really means allowing the decisions to be made by people closest to the product and the customer, maybe 10 percent of our organizations are doing it. We're caught between these two paradigms.

What this really means is that the bureaucratic structure doesn't encourage risk taking; it doesn't encourage chaos, which many organizations have to live with. It doesn't encourage leaders who shake up the system, who make waves, who rock the boat. Most bureaucracies like reasonable, adaptive, malleable, docile people.

George Bernard Shaw once said, "All progress depends on the unreasonable man." Most organizations are filled with reasonable people who adapt to the world, instead of forcing the world to adapt to them. One of the problems I had in helping select a new president for the University of Southern California, interestingly enough, was finding candidates who would shake up the system, because there's no organization today that can be docile or complacent. There's no organization today that I can think of that is in a stable environment where you can really talk about a long-range plan with any certainty.

I think the move from the old paradigm to the new paradigm is going to take time and won't be smooth. For the organizations that don't move in this direction, it's going to be death on the installment plan. Because, unless organizations change in the direction we're talking about here, they're just going to be beaten by competitors.

Townsend: Before we go any further, I understand what you mean about empowerment, which is giving the people in the forty square feet where the work is done the power to do it and to make changes, without having to go to their supervisor or anybody else. What do you mean by acknowledge and create?

Bennis: Acknowledgment really has a lot of different meanings. It means everything from praise such as a "Way to go!" when someone does a decent job, to celebrating victories, to creating an environment where people really feel understood, where the reward system seems to be consistent and congruent and corresponds to the organizational vision. People really feel appreciated for what they do. That's what I mean by acknowledgment.

Create is sort of a buzzword that I use for initiative, autonomy, doing the right thing without having to ask permission. Perhaps I'm being oversimplistic, but I think the world of control, order, and predict is one that today, despite all the rhetoric, still dominates most of our institutions.

Let me try to start off with how we get from A to B, from the COP paradigm to the ACE paradigm. A lot of it's got to do with unlearning; a lot of it's got to do with how executives not only take on certain behaviors or attitudes, but unlearn things that were successful in the past. If there's one thing that I hear a lot of as I go around talking to corporate executives and top leaders, it's "How do I get people who have been successful in the past to change in ways that are also going to be successful in the future?" If they continue doing things the way they've been doing them, they're not going to succeed in the next five years.

One example I would give of a leader who's trying to move from the COP paradigm to the acknowledge, create, and empower paradigm is Bob Haas, who's chairman and CEO of Levi Strauss—one of my favorite companies and one of my favorite leaders. He said not long ago that the difficult thing is to unlearn behaviors that made us successful in the past.[2] For example, I've got to learn to listen rather than speak. I've got to learn to value people of different genders or from different cultures rather than just value people like myself. I've got to unlearn doing things on my own and I've got to learn to do more collaborating and cooperating. I've got to learn to ask different people for their perspectives rather than just making the decision myself.

Now, how do you get leaders to want to learn things? I think there are a number of things that can lead people

2. Paraphrase of Haas's comments in Warren Bennis, ed., *Leaders on Leadership: Interviews with Top Executives* (Boston: Harvard Business School Press, 1992), p. 44.

from one paradigm to the other, but I'd like your reaction to that, Bob.

Townsend: Well, my reaction to that Bob Haas example is that Levi Strauss went through a great crisis, didn't it? Its business all but disappeared or looked like it was going to disappear. And we get back to the value of a crisis, in getting leaders to think about their behavior and to discuss the matter with the rest of the organization and to get the rest of the organization to pay attention and tell them what they have to learn or unlearn. Not everybody will have a crisis that severe. But I guess the lesson from that crisis is, whatever crisis you've got, and don't tell me you haven't had a crisis, use it to change from COP to ACE.

Bennis: When we talk about high-performing systems and good organizations today, most people talk about the Four Fs. Rosabeth Moss Kanter is perhaps the best expositor of this. She said, "Organizations should be . . . fast, focused, flexible and friendly. But they also ought to be fun." This is why you see beer busts, or you see leaders clowning. I think there are ways of making the environment fun and more spirited rather than simply dull, bleak, and barren. I think leaders can have something to do with that spirit, the tone of the company. They need to put a light spin on things and not get into that repetitive, monotonous bureaucratization of the imagination.

Townsend: And it can be one on one. It doesn't have to be beer busts. Just the consistent demonstration of a sense of humor in times of adversity will get through the grapevine and begin to characterize the whole organization.

Bennis: Yes, yes. I can give a recent example . . .

Townsend: Sure.

Bennis: At a lot of universities, the students have what's called a confidential guide, which is a survey of how students feel about their professors. In the recent confidential guide, it was said about one of our professors, who's a very distinguished man, that he's such a bad lecturer he ought to go out and shoot himself. The next day he comes into this huge lecture room, Economics 101, with something like seven hundred students, and he strides up to the podium in the center of the auditorium and he takes out a toy pistol and points it at his head and goes "Pop!" That simple gesture just broke the ice and made him more human. I'm not sure he improved as a lecturer but his actions indicated, at least, that he was listening.

Townsend: I've got one comment on this business of not taking yourself too seriously or building your whole life on your position. When Avis became sort of famous as a turnaround phenomenon, as CEO, I got much more credit than I deserved. Visitors used to come see me. The chairman of our British company, who I'll call Lord Curmudgeon, came over to pay a visit. He arrived and our receptionist in the lobby called me and said, "Lord Curmudgeon is here," and I said, "Wheel him in." At that time we were so proud of our troops in the field that we had two jackets, blue and red, that the executives were wearing at headquarters. On that day I was wearing the red one, an Eisenhower jacket that just came down to the end of the rib cage. That was the jacket our service agents wore in the field. I walked out in the hall and welcomed Lord Curmudgeon and walked back with him. We got into a discussion and I called in the treasurer, Dick Pine, because he was getting into questions that I couldn't answer. Then my visitor asked another question, which required a memo, so I said, "Dick, you continue the conversation with Lord Curmudgeon and I'll go get that memo." I walked out to get it in somebody else's office. And Lord Curmudgeon turned to Dick Pine and said, "Is he *really* the chairman?" Well, things like that are fairly good for keeping your self-esteem from getting out of control. By the way, Louis Gerstner, the new CEO of IBM, is wearing cardigans around the "crystal palace," which was famous for its strict dress code in the good old days. Sometimes the best way a leader can communicate is nonverbal—by simply making a minor change in his or her routine.

Dialogue Starters

1. **PARTNER ANALYSIS:** Using a hypothetical project, discuss how it will evolve. One of you takes the approach of a leader using the COP paradigm; the other takes the approach of a leader who uses the ACE paradigm. Is there a difference in how effective each approach will be? Be open to both approaches; it's not a given that the ACE paradigm will work better for you unless your whole organization is structured to enforce it.

2. **LISTING EXERCISE:** List all the behaviors that you feel have contributed to your development as a leader. Now list the opposites of these behaviors. Can you see how unlearning what you have learned might be helpful to further empower your organization? List how this new set of behaviors could make a difference, then evaluate which behavior is most useful to you.

Chapter 8

Overcoming Crisis

Probably one of the most challenging elements of a leader's job is to manage crisis situations effectively. If handled poorly, a crisis situation can cause a company to take a downward plunge. If handled well, crisis management can be used to make needed changes in an organization. Crisis allows the company vision to be tested. If the vision holds up under fire, it becomes stronger and more meaningful to all the stakeholders.

This chapter offers a few techniques to help you navigate your way through this potentially harrowing situation. You'll learn how empowerment is an important part of crisis management and how it also ensures that your followers and customers profit from individuals who take charge. You'll also discover why developing the complex relationship skills of a master politician while maintaining a generalist's perspective can pave the way to the most effective form of leadership. Overcoming crisis can provide opportunities for doing things and solving problems in new ways . . . ways that will bring you closer to realizing the company vision.

—ROBERT TOWNSEND

How can companies handle crises successfully and use them to foster change?

Bennis: After Volkswagen was reeling from a three-quarters-of-a-billion-dollar drop in its profits in 1993, the chairman, Ferdinand Piech, decided on a plan of drastic action. He suggested altering the way the company builds its cars, slashing employment, and keeping down the high prices VW pays suppliers. This was at the time the company was also having problems with one of its employees who had jumped ship at GM and was accused of taking valuable trade secrets with him to VW. Piech stood firmly behind this guy, J. Ignacio Lopez de Arriortua, and accused GM of trying to discredit his company. By July of that year, the company was reporting a $40 million profit.

Another example of an even more dramatic crisis occurred after the World Trade Center bombing when the accounting firm of Deloitte and Touche was forced out of the towers in late February, right in the heart of tax season. The group managing partner of the New York office, William Parrett, made the decision to place ads immediately in the media to contact workers and get them to call the headquarters. Only one hundred responded. The director of human resources then assigned staff to contact every one of the twenty-two hundred employees of the firm and offer them trauma counseling. All the employees pulled together to get the firm up and running again.

Those are two examples where crisis was used successfully to get the business back on the right track. But in both cases, I should point out, these companies used one of the qualities of leadership we mentioned before—inclusion.Volkswagen, while playing it rough, tried to work together with its suppliers to make changes that would be beneficial to everyone in the industry. The same thing was true of Deloitte and Touche. It reached out to its employees, then included them in its decision making, rather than circling the wagons and keeping a tight lip, which too many organizations do in a crisis. The usual response in a crisis is to regress, to close down.

When people get anxious, they typically narrow down what they hear. All information channels seem to be on overload. Companies that are really successful, that transcend crisis and profit from it, and transform themselves as a result in a productive way, are those that include more and more voices.

Townsend: I've got one example for you of a company that faced a crisis. Brunswick lost a third of its business when it eliminated its medical division; there was great disaffection among those on the board of directors and the president quit. Jack Reichert became chief executive officer. His philosophy was: Wealth is created in the divisions, not at headquarters. He scrapped the whole group concept, which eliminated a layer of management and four hundred positions. He reduced the corporate staff by two thirds. He moved the division managers to the field. He froze senior management pay and tied it to profits. Then he did something that he said was the most important thing—it's the "E" of ACE. He quintupled capital expenditure authority from top to bottom of the organization. If a supervisor had a $100 approval limit to buy tools, it became $500; if a vice-president had a $10,000 approval limit for a capital expenditure, it became $50,000. He said increasing this authority did more to convince people that he trusted them and was seriously trying to create a better company than anything else. He also gave each employee nine shares of stock. Two years later Brunswick was a different company: exciting, leaner, peppier, financially stronger, more productive. Stock went way up. The general feeling was "We get more work done with fewer people." That's one response of a leader.

Bennis: If I can return for a moment to the subject of empowerment, that part of what you just said is really interesting. One of the things that Max De Pree does is insist that workers, after they've been there ninety days, buy stock in the company. I think the issue of ownership is so important when we talk about empowerment. The best metaphor I can think of is how people feel about the cars they rent versus the cars they own. Have you ever seen anyone wash a rent-a-car? I think that was brilliant of Reichert.

Let me give you another example of transformation that has gone on, actually, over the last eight or nine years. This is also an example of a leader whom I respect very much. He's Jan Carlzon, the CEO of Scandinavian Airlines System. SAS is a really complex organization, because it's owned by three countries: Norway, Denmark, and Sweden. And it's got hubs in all three of those countries. The headquarters is in Stockholm, the training center is in Copenhagen, and a lot of executive offices are in Oslo. Interesting company.

Jan is one of the most interesting executives I've ever come across. He transformed an organization that was losing between $20 million and $25 million yearly, back in the late seventies and early eighties, into a company that in 1993 was worth over $5 billion. It was a company that was just barely getting along, and in a short time—six years—he did a magnificent job with it. And the transformation is still happening. He established and created a vision in a lot of different ways: from eyeballing it with employees to writing a marvelous cartoon book that also echoed the vision he had for the company.

But, most of all, his dream was interesting. His dream was to offer premium service. He would pick his passengers up in a limo or one of those super shuttle buses and give them their boarding pass; when they arrived at their destination, they would be given the keys to the hotel room and the luggage would be in the room when they got there. They wouldn't even have to check in.

Now when he told me this dream, I couldn't suppress a laugh. And he said, "You don't think it's possible?" I said, "No, I don't." He said, "Well, we've been doing this for our crews for the last forty years." Interesting.

That was his dream, but he had a whole set of interrelated aspects of that dream. If he wanted SAS to become one of the world's greatest airlines, and there are only going to be seven or eight of them, he would have to attract business class. And in order to attract business class, he would have to make things better by 1 percent in a hundred different ways. Notice he didn't say he wanted to be 100 percent better in one way, but to be 1 percent better in a hundred different ways. Then he said something really interesting. He said, "Look, I've estimated, based on a lot of reports, that SAS employees have roughly sixty-three thousand interactions with customers or potential customers every single day—sixty-three thousand customer contacts. I call those 'moments of truth.' If we can endow every single one of those moments of truth with caring and courtesy, and real relevance for customers or future customers, we're going to get business."

Now, I like the dream. I like the ideas he has. But in order to actually implement or anchor that dream, to manage the dream, he had to do a lot of things. He had to start recruiting differently. He said, "By and large, if you're going to have people connecting with the public, you better get extroverts. They like talking to people. They like interacting with people. Don't get introverts. They don't like to do that." So he recruited meticulously. He rewarded good service. He set up a corporate leadership program in Copenhagen where every executive, every employee—there were twelve thousand when they started—had to go through that leadership school one week a year.

By the way, the title of the book he wrote in Swedish is *Destroying the Pyramid*. The most dramatic thing he did and the one that's most problematic and controversial was that he took that old bureaucratic structure, COP, and he based his new organization on route structure. For example, on the Copenhagen–New York route, which is the biggest and most profitable, every single person, from the food caterers to the people who clean the cabin, to the airline pilots, to the mechanics, to the flight attendants, to the reservation clerks, works in a self-managed work team. And this includes unions.

So it's a gain-sharing system, it's a profit-sharing system, and it's a cost center. If you look now at an organizational chart of SAS, it looks like a galaxy of different kinds of pods or spokes coming out from a hub based on these route structures. It's really incredible.

Finally, Carlzon had to create alliances with hotels, with other airlines, if he was to be truly global and international. So over the last five years he has bought a controlling interest in Continental Airlines, with lots of gates in Newark, and he's bought a controlling interest in hotels so he can execute and manage that dream.

Now, think of all the things he's done. This is another example of a guy who came in who was able to transform an organization and it's still evolving.

Townsend: You can hear in his ads his attempt to empower his employees. He says, "All of our people are empowered to make decisions. If you have a complaint, complain to the nearest person—a flight attendant perhaps—and you'll get instant satisfaction, because we all have the power to handle problems." And employees will make decisions. The problem won't go through five layers of supervision and come back a month later in the form of a letter from the chairman.

Dialogue Starters

1. BRAINSTORMING DIALOGUE: Get together with at least one person and brainstorm small steps you can take to

transform some of the problem areas in your organization. Make sure you include the word *empower* in your answer.

2. WHAT-IF DISCUSSION: Do you know how your company would react if there was a major crisis—one of the magnitude, say, that Johnson and Johnson faced as a result of the Tylenol incident? Is there a common vision it could adhere to? How would you involve the stakeholders? Who would most likely be in charge of handling the crisis? Would your company take an inclusive approach? Perhaps you might suggest staging a crisis practice session where you could plan for future emergency situations.

How can someone be an effective leader when managing a crisis?

Bennis: Leaders at every single level of the organization are going to have to develop a lot more, excuse the jargon, cognitive complexity. They're going to have to think like a kaleidoscope. That is, they're going to have to look at many different patterns and combinations that form a picture of the whole organization. They're going to have to think about the word *systems* in a different way than we talked about earlier. Not systems that confine, but systems that we really have to take into account. I think it's going to take a great deal more thinking about what's going on with various stakeholders.

One change in the way leaders do business today that I've noticed, and that I like, is that they are really trying to develop a lot of different partnerships. I'm not just talking about the joint ventures you referred to earlier. I'm talking about creating partnerships within the firm. Every person in a firm I know about, by the way, is either a supplier or a buyer. So, in a typical firm, you're not dealing with a hierarchy, you're dealing with people who can do something for you or people who can't. So then the work of a leader, more and more, is to see relationships and contingencies and complexity. All of these things.

We talked about Jim Burke earlier and how he dealt with the Tylenol crisis. In dealing with that crisis he had to take into account a number of different stakeholders, a number of different audiences. He had to take into account the customers; he had to take into account the doctors; he had to take into account the community. He had to take into account the shareholders, unions, and a lot of other things in dealing with that situation.

Successful leaders have to be able to think constructively about complexity so they can have some stakeholder symmetry, or equity among stakeholders. They have to take into account a lot more stakeholders than they ever dreamed of thirty or forty years ago. Somebody once said, "Seek simplicity and then distrust it." The world we're living in is more cluttered than we like, and we have to not *confine* it but *define* it, and be clear about it. But that's going to take a lot of kaleidoscopic thinking.

Townsend: I know what you mean, but I can't leave you where you stopped. More stakeholders? Yes. More complexity? Absolutely. But kaleidoscopic thinking? I don't like that image. If you mean we have to consider many different patterns before picking a systems solution, then certainly I agree. But let's not abandon simplicity. Most of the elegant solutions I'm familiar with came about from worrying at the layers of complexity and peeling the onion until—eureka—a simpler solution appeared. It doesn't always work, but when it does, we're glad we spent the time using clear linear thinking for each layer of complexity. Does that make sense?

Bennis: Again, I like playing back and forth between simplicity and complexity, because I think in order to get things reduced to simplicity, one needs to be profound. Here's an oxymoron: I think what you're talking about is "profound simplicity." In order to really make anything simple you've got to understand the complexity of it.

Bill Parcells, former head coach of the New York Giants and current head coach of the New England Patriots, when he was asked what coaching was all about, said something in simple language. He said, "Coaching is giving your team a good design and getting them to play hard." Right? I mean who would argue with that? Isn't it profound? It's profound simplicity, not simplistic. I'm always amazed at truth; it always sounds simple but it comes out of so much experience and complexity.

Townsend: And if we're going to agree that Bill Parcells is a good example of a leader, then we go back to our second point on the list of "intelligent, articulate." That doesn't mean overintelligent or overarticulate. Parcells's statement is not overarticulate. It just happens to be a simple, true, honest statement, which is all that's required of any chief executive.

Bennis: I think specialized management is an enemy of hope and of good management. I think what we need, if anything, is deep generalists. I think business schools have played into specialization too much because you get fractionalized or you get compartmentalized. That's a disservice to institutions. I think leaders have to have a holistic view of the situation. The best example I can give you is one I heard about during my days as a university president. A dean of a medical school was decrying the specialization of medicine. He said, "My God, you have to go to about five different doctors to get taken care of. The only generalist we have left in the hospital today is the patient." I think specialization has really been the enemy of hope. Business schools have had a hand in this and I think it's dangerous.

I think everyone should have a specialty. I really believe that one *should* have a discipline. But it has to be far broader. That's what I mean by *deep generalists,* people with maybe a discipline that they came out of, but who can also see the big picture.

But they certainly have learned a whole business. As a matter of fact, the very best leaders I've come across know every aspect of that business; they have business literacy. If they're in the publishing business they know how the presses work, they know about the technology of printing, they know about distribution. The failures I've seen are people who are just so specialized that they just can't see the forest for the trees.

Townsend: If you're running some part of a company, a few useful questions to ask yourself are these: Are my people excited? Are they energetic? Are they creative? Are they free to make mistakes? And if not, what's chaining them? What's restraining them? What in the organization can I get rid of that will free them to be as creative and energetic and excited as they can be?

To me, the answer has always been the same in all the organizations I've worked in. There is a structure that has just grown up in the organization that is tolerated by everybody. In many cases this structure is still growing. What it does is impinge on the lives and the energies and the creativity of people. I know you're tired of hearing about it, but the PR Department, the Human Resources Department if unrestrained, the Management Information System Department if unrestrained, will impinge on the activities of your people, interrupt them, force them on committees they don't want to be on, force them to write and respond to memoranda they don't want to deal with, force them to attend meetings they don't want to go to. This kind of activity chains people's spirits and makes it difficult to remain energetic. One of the leader's jobs is to free people from their burdens and get them focused on the vision of the company.

Once they're focused and energetic and excited, the need for control almost disappears. They're doing their thing. They know what's expected of them, they're being rewarded, their progress is being measured, and the feedback to them is up-to-date and frequent. This frees the leader to concentrate on the horizon and the obstacles and the opportunities that are looming ahead and to be thinking about the next vision.

Dialogue Starters

1. **DEBATE QUESTION: Is it better to manage with a sense of complexity or simplicity, especially during a crisis? One partner expresses the opinion that in order to be an effective leader, it's important to have a kaleidoscopic vision of a company and pay attention to the needs of all the stakeholders. The other partner takes the view that boiling things down to their most basic element and eliminating**

the layers is the best way to handle challenges.

2. LISTING EXERCISE: Do you seek to be a generalist or a specialist? List the areas of your company that you don't know much about. Now list the aspects of your department you don't know much about. Evaluate whether learning about other areas will improve your job performance.

Chapter 9

Thriving Where the Treasure Lies

Failure is perhaps the best learning experience anyone can hope to achieve. For it is only through failure, and even through the risk of failure, that you can apply the new information you receive, and increase your chances for success the next time. It is important for you, as a leader, to teach your followers the importance of making mistakes and how not to be afraid of obstacles. Norman Lear once said, "To be an effective leader, you not only have to get the group of followers on the right path, but you must be able to convince them that whatever obstacle stands in the way ahead, whether it's a tree or a building that blocks the view, you're going to get around it."

In this chapter, we'll address the subject of mistakes and how leaders can learn to make mistakes and still be effective. When mistakes are made, learning how to handle them is the most sensitive and crucial area for a leader. You'll also learn the importance of leaders' taking the blame, and how loyalty can be built with a creative approach to reviewing mistakes. Ultimately, the most important thing a leader can do when mistakes are made is to empower his or her followers to handle them. The notion of risk is inherent in the nature of mistakes. It's important to know how to encourage risks and how to make your organization more risk-prone. Risks are valuable, for as Lear also believed, "Everywhere you trip is where the treasure lies."

—WARREN BENNIS

At what point does a leader really learn from his or her mistakes?

Bennis: All the executives I've gotten to know really well felt that when they hit bottom, when they really screwed up, that's when they learned the most. This notion was confirmed by a major study that was done recently on successful leaders. It was Margaret Thatcher who said, "It's at that moment when the iron entered my soul that gave me the steel I needed to have the resilience to become a really first-rate leader." I like that phrase: It's at that moment when the iron entered my soul. So I cannot exaggerate the significance of people's learning from failure and having an opportunity to reflect upon their experiences.

Townsend: I could not agree more. Perhaps the best way to illustrate this point is with an exaggeration. Let's say you're a CEO and I come running in with some bad news and you blow up and fire me. Can you imagine what effect that has on the organization, how much truth you're going to get from then on? Organizations have to make mistakes.

They have to admit them; they have to fix them. Leaders don't have to rejoice about these mistakes but they certainly have to allow their employees to make and learn from mistakes, and it helps to laugh about them.

Now the real question is, why do we have so many organizations where you're not allowed to make mistakes or you're afraid to make mistakes? If top management acts like it's infallible, then the feedback from its decisions has to be repackaged. It has to be reshaped or denied. In any case, management isn't correcting its mistakes. As John Cleese mentions, you can't say, "Well, I did that right, so now I better fix it." You just can't say that. If the top of the organization is that way, the bottom will never admit mistakes. Management will cover them up and then they don't get fixed. And the whole organization, if it's a business organization, will self-destruct.

People think they're experts in three fields. One is their own field, whatever it is. The second is writing advertising copy. And the third is behavioral science, which is your field. So I will fearlessly jump into your field and tell you why people are so afraid of mistakes.

We all have egos. Egos are wounded when somebody says to us, "You're wrong." Some people have more fragile egos than others, so they go to great lengths to avoid being wounded. They think about what they're going to say six times before they say it and make sure that nobody's ever going to accuse them of saying something wrong.

Well, in doing that, they remove all spontaneity, all creativity, and what they say is so safe that it's useless. Again, to use John Cleese's great example, he says, "If you asked me what time it was, I could tell you that it was between eight A.M. and noon, and nobody could fault me on that,

117

but it's not very useful. On the other hand, I could say it's ten twenty-four, and I might be wrong by a minute or two, but it would be a lot more useful to you than the first.''

To be creative in our organizations, we must be able to say and do things that we haven't thought all the way through, and don't know about; things that might look like mistakes and might be mistakes. Nothing creative is done when people are fearful of being accused of being wrong or making a mistake.

You must be ready to say and do things that are foolish or turn out to be foolish. Now there's one kind of mistake that's different—you don't want to launch the Edsel, you don't want to start a land war in Asia. But for most things, you don't know that they're mistakes until you're well into them. And then the key thing in a healthy organization is to admit them fast, admit them widely, and get them fixed so you can laugh about them and go on with the learning process.

The way to convince yourself and your followers to make mistakes, which is part of empowerment, is to say, ''Look at the mistake. We all have egos, they're all centrally located, they all can be bruised. Think of it this way. If I admit my mistake as soon as I recognize it, before I've studied it and realize how bad it is and have figured out all the reasons and excuses, if I just say, 'I made a mistake, help me fix it,' I'm doing that with the least amount of pain to my ego.''

And offsetting that pain is the reward of getting a reputation in the company as somebody who admits it when he's wrong. There aren't many of those. That almost cancels out the pain of saying, ''I made a mistake.''

If you do that, you're going to inflict less pain on yourself than if you cover up the mistake and then wait while it becomes bigger, and finally enormous pain is inflicted by saying, "I not only made a mistake, but then I made two more mistakes by covering it up and denying it." So please, get this idea in your head, in your people's heads, that the best thing to do is try something. When you decide you've made a mistake, admit the mistake, ask for help if you need it, and correct your error. Then your organization, your part of it at least, will be healthy. It will be a learning organization. You'll be a hero and your people will be heroes and empowered.

Bennis: I don't see how you can have a successful organization today without creating a risk-prone environment. There's no such thing as a safe risk. In this environment where innovation is going to make the key difference, where trying new things can give you a competitive advantage, I don't see any other alternative. If you look at the most successful companies, they do try to create an environment that is risk-prone.

My favorite example is the 3M company. There, you'll find three examples that demonstrate the company's commitment to allowing others to make mistakes. First, its motto, which I like, is tolerate failure. Second, it has a company policy that 25 percent of sales has to come from products that have been created in the lab within the last five years. Actually 3M just changed that to three years, which I think is pretty tough. Third, it has an innovation fund for employees to do pilot programs that are outrageous and that everyone thinks are crazy. The area where these programs take place was sometimes referred to as the Cockamamie Center, where crazy ideas are not only floated, but encouraged.

I don't think an organization has any choice right now

but to embrace a new era, to take a risk. If it doesn't it's just not going to change. Leaders are change agents.

I've always asked three questions of every leader I've interviewed over the last thirteen years, and that's about 150 of them. First, what are your strengths and weaknesses? Second, what was the most significant experience in your development as a leader? And third, can you tell me about your career path and the choices you made and why you decided to stay or not stay in a job?

Townsend: I suppose the kaleidoscopic thinkers you interviewed tried to answer all three questions at the same time? Just teasing. I really hate that kaleidoscopic image.

Bennis: I won't mention the word *kaleidoscopic* again until you're out of earshot. Now, what I've discovered among all of these leaders is that first of all, failure screams out for explanation. Reflective, thoughtful, successful people, as you said earlier, try to really look at that, and not always assign blame to somebody else, but really try to understand their role in what happened. Then they feel free to talk about their mistakes, admit them, and try to learn from the experience.

I can give you example after example. Barbara Corday, a big television writer and producer, had two awful events happen in her life in one week. Her husband left her and she lost her job. Love and work together, you know? Powerful. She said she learned more from that than anything else that's ever happened to her.

Mike McGee, athletic director at USC, said the most significant thing that happened to him was when he was fired as head football coach at Duke.

Kay Graham, the former publisher of *The Washington*

Post, said, "For me a mistake is simply another way of doing things."

In every single case, I'm not just talking about the organization, which you were emphasizing, I'm talking about personal growth. Failure screams out for explanation. Those who are successful learn from mistakes and failure.

Dialogue Starters

1. GROUP DIALOGUE: **How does your place of business handle mistakes? Do you know of any major ones that were made within the company? How were they handled? What if someone in your organization were to take a big risk—would people frown upon it or encourage it? Is there a difference between who is allowed to take risks and who isn't? Why? How could you promote a more risk-prone atmosphere in your office?**

2. BRAINSTORMING DIALOGUE: **Discuss brainstorming sessions at your company. How is innovation treated? Are people allowed to express their ideas in a noncritical environment? Brainstorm ways your people can offer new ideas without being attacked. Now brainstorm ways people can be free to make mistakes without repercussions.**

What is the most important quality a leader needs to handle mistakes in a company?

Bennis: When Apple Computer first launched its Newton MessagePad, it was widely ridiculed by consumers and the press. The company had to regroup, and seven months later it issued a new, cheaper, and more useful version in an attempt to overcome many of the shortcomings of the original. At that time, one of the company vice-presidents, Gaston Bastiaens, said simply, "We listened to our customers and adapted to their requests." The company's vision, demonstrated by its concern for its customers; its integrity, demonstrated by its honest and hard look at what was wrong with the product; and its courage in admitting it had made a mistake are examples of what to do when faced with a difficult situation.

If you want to look at what Perrier did when it was discovered that its bottled mineral water was contaminated by the chemical benzene—the company spent a year denying there was a problem. Or look at the *Valdez* disaster, which the leadership at Exxon initially dealt with in a less than forthcoming manner. So vision, integrity, and courage are all important qualities.

Townsend: One example of a mistake where leadership didn't demonstrate integrity and was hurt as a result was when American Express had its salad oil scandal. A lot of investment banks owned American Express Field Warehousing Corporation receipts backed by salad oil in tanks over in New Jersey, and all of a sudden it was discovered that the tanks were empty and the paper was no good. And American Express did not make good on that paper. That error cost the company many millions of dollars. All American Express said was "Oops, we never bothered to check those tanks. Sorry about that, but that wasn't us. It was a wholly owned subsidiary using our name and we're sorry but that subsidiary doesn't have any assets." And the company made good on maybe only 70 percent of its investments, but 30 percent of these investments were down the drain. Several firms, including H. Hentz and Company, went belly up as a result of that decision.

Bennis: A danger in handling mistakes is when the top people come in and arrogate to themselves the responsibilities of the people who have been working on the problem. I recognized this when, over twenty years ago, I was doing some consulting for the State Department. Anytime a mistake happened in an area, the area director would take over from the country director and suddenly the secretary of state was doing all the work; that really demoralized the people who had knowledge of the problem, who were closest to the problem. This technique for handling problems really destroyed the structure of the organization and demoralized everyone involved.

That's probably one of the dangers of managing problems, where you take on the roles of those individuals who have been used to working on the problem and who are pretty good at their jobs.

Townsend: And what you've done in addition to arrogating the responsibility, you've probably made sure that the decisions will be worse. You've demoralized the people who should have been given a chance to grow.

Bennis: Right. By not delegating responsibility, you train people to be docile and reactive. And when the next crisis comes along, it's "just phone headquarters."

I would think that when you review problems, you're better off. Let's say as a result of a series of mistakes, you experienced a very consequential failure. I would like to see the executive team take a look and determine what went wrong. Maybe the person in charge would say, "It isn't just my fault as a leader; let's diagnose what happened." That may mean that you look at a variety of different parts of the system where things may have been screwed up. And you aren't the only one to take the blame for what happened.

I figured that out when I had to resign as vice-president of a university because I no longer felt that my voice counted and some very significant decisions were made against what I thought was my better judgment. I resigned during the student turmoil in 1970, and I made a loud, noisy exit. When I became president of another university, I had a problem with subordinates of mine, some of the vice-presidents and deans who I felt did the wrong thing, but I could never publicly indicate that they had messed up. In fact I had to be the fall guy. I didn't like this role particularly, nor did I always publicly take the blame, but I would never point the finger in public at any person reporting to me directly or indirectly.

But I always wondered, if I really disagreed with what someone did, which got the university into trouble, why I couldn't say, "Yes, he messed up and we're going to talk about it." That would have been the honest thing, but publicly I never could do that. I think what you're saying, Bob, is that this is the price of leadership.

Townsend: I think it is the price, because obviously you're going to talk to him privately about it. And all you have to do is consider how the conversation's going to go if he's read his name in the paper with you saying "He messed up." You know? He's not going to listen to you.

Bennis: That's right.

Townsend: So you're defeating yourself.

Bennis: By the way, I think that taking the blame publicly is a very interesting action and one that you never read about.

Townsend: No, and it's very important, I think, to help your people grow and get empowered. If they are belabored by these unseen, powerful forces from way upstairs in the organization, or outside in the media, they become terrified. You don't know how terrified they are.

Bennis: I suppose there are times when a controlled anger might not be inappropriate, and at a point in time when things are going on in a way that will ultimately hurt the institution, there may be grounds for expressing anger. It's another way of kicking the Coke machine; if it's not out of control, it could really open people's minds up to "Look, we've really got to get moving on this."

Townsend: Yes, I can see in a case where a leader who assumes that he's earned enough trust to get the truth discovers that he hasn't heard the truth. Nobody brought him the bad news until it was too late and too expensive. He could get justifiably angry. But not so angry as to be destructive. You'll remember the great IBM example when some individual made a $10 million mistake and went in to see his boss and said, "I assume I'm fired."

Bennis: I think it was Tom Watson he went to.

Townsend: Watson Senior or Junior?

Bennis: I think it was Watson Junior.

Townsend: And Watson said, "Are you crazy? We've just invested ten million dollars in your education. Do you think we're gonna let an asset like that get out of the company?" Which is a trust-building experience. Talk about loyalty.

Dialogue Starters

1. **PARTNER ANALYSIS: Have your partner analyze your ability to maintain integrity in times of crisis. What other qual-**

ities do you possess that would help you to be a good leader when mistakes have been made? Are you able to communicate those qualities to your followers?

2. DEFINITION EXERCISE: What does empowerment in times of difficulty mean to you? Do you tend to arrogate or delegate responsibilities? Define some of the ways you could be a more empowering leader to your employees in a difficult situation. How often do you take the blame for others? If you don't, list some of the benefits this action might have for your employees.

Chapter 10

Strategies for the New Work Paradigm

Language and cultural diversity, gender and color bias, leaving your organization or enlisting new leaders in your cause—these aren't new subjects in the world of business. But today's challenges make yesterday's challenges pale in comparison.

The mere "manager" works fine when the environment is stable and the organization is prosperous. But these are new times, and they demand new solutions from leaders. With ever-changing technology, increased globalization, and greater demographic diversity, leadership requires new skills and new paradigms. In this chapter, we'll explore what these new challenges mean for today's leader, how to keep up with these changes, and how to make changes gracefully within your own organization. That includes a discussion on choosing a leader for the organization— common traps to avoid, why the "obvious choice" isn't always the right choice, and when leaders should take time out for rest and reflection.

—ROBERT TOWNSEND

What effects will a changing environment have on providing good leadership?

Bennis: I don't think there's an organization today that is immune to a certain number of forces affecting its environment. And that's why the move from the old paradigm to the one we've been talking about is so critical. Because we aren't living in a stable, unchanging, complacent economy, and you can't predict today what's going to happen two or three years down the road.

Two major events that I can recall took place during my early career as a professor at MIT. One was a northeast power failure, and the other was the Cuban missile crisis. I often have the nightmare, what if those disasters had happened at the same time? We would have probably been plunged into World War III. Crises, back then, came in pairs like FBI agents. But now they come in multiples of four, five, and six.

There were no management books in those days, which may have been a blessing in disguise. The only management book that I recall having taken a look at during my graduate school days, believe it or not, was a book by J. Paul Getty, his autobiography. This book more than any other will demonstrate the change between now and then. He had three rules for success in business. They were (1) get up early; (2) work hard; and (3) find oil.

I conduct a CEO conference every six weeks or so and we bring in interesting speakers like Tom Peters and others of his stature. We had one conference on religion in America and I invited the cardinal of Los Angeles and Harvey Cox, who teaches religion at Harvard. I wanted to get the Dalai Lama, thinking we'd have a nice ecumenical program. I sent a friend of mine who's Indian to visit the Dalai Lama, with a letter from me, inviting him to this seminar on religion. A month later, I got back a letter saying he couldn't come. But what's interesting about the way he communicated the letter is that it came through the USC fax machine. Now, imagine the Dalai Lama, sitting atop the Himalayas and sending back a fax message to me. I think that says something about technology. The fact is that it's changing the world in ways that we could never, ever foresee.

Technology means globalization; 88 percent of all U.S. products have at least one foreign component. According to Peter Sprague, who's the head of National Semiconductor, Russians work on product research, the chips are designed in Israel, the semiconductors are manufactured here in the States, and they're assembled in Asia. Now are those U.S. products or not?

Anyway, how can one be blind to these forces of demographic diversity, technology, and globalization? I don't think this change is a secret or mystery to anybody who's working in a large organization. No company can hide right now from the forces of globalization. Among the top leaders I've known, almost all of them have had some international experience or some experience equivalent to being international.

Townsend: Talking about globalization brings up the question of language. I don't believe a leader should have to be able to speak a foreign language. We're American businesses and we should never forget that.

Bennis: And thank God the language of business is English. So, we're pretty lucky.

Townsend: Right, we're lucky. Our employees have to learn English and there's no question about that in my mind. They can be Hispanic, Arab, Asian, whatever, but they're going to have to learn it if they're going to succeed in any organization that I approve of.

Bennis: Spoken by an old English major. Our background and discipline often do determine the way we're going to be later on.

Townsend: Well, I majored in English, but I've taken pains to be semifluent in French and Spanish, so I'm not speaking subjectively. But there's one thing beyond everything we've discussed to date that a leader has to have. In addition to being gender-blind and color-blind as an individual, the leader has to be aware of the possibility of race or gender discrimination that will exist in any company and the hostility toward people of color and women in the organization. Hopefully, we can defeat racism and sexism. But it's with us for now, and any competent leader should be prepared to tackle these tough and important issues.

Bennis: Isn't it ironic that military institutions have probably advanced more in this area, in regard to both gender and race, than the civilian population?

Townsend: Yes, the military has. But I'm not sure that average companies can adopt the military's approach. My answer to the question "Shouldn't management put some statement about racism into the concrete or the Lucite in the lobby?'' is ''No.'' The leader's actions will speak louder than words and nothing need be said beyond actions that indicate the attitude of the company.

And one of the great things about organizations is that it's still ''monkey see, monkey do.'' If the leader is color-blind, race-blind, and gender-blind, these attitudes will be passed on to other people. Written statements are counterproductive. They just give rise to jokes—counterproductive jokes.

With respect to the question of changing jobs, this has been the ''white-knuckle decade.'' We all know enormous numbers of people who are being given early retirement or laid off. It's not a nice time to go job hunting, because the number of people looking for work is increasing while the number of good jobs seems to be shrinking.

There are a lot of people who have become entrepreneurs and are self-employed; there are some good things about that. But my experience has always been that you can have fun in even the worst organizations. And you just have to figure out what you can do that's in your nature and in your style that will be profitable for the organization, in line with whatever goals and objectives the company has, and that will still permit you and the people you manage to grow, learn, and have fun. Figure out how you can have fun where you are. That's what I'd do in the white-knuckle decade.

Bennis: I often have people asking me about situations they're in and whether they should leave or stay and how can they improve the situation should they stay. It's very tough for me to answer these questions because I don't know their situations specifically. But quite often I tell people, ''Look, as you tell me about your situation, as I understand it, you've got no other recourse but to move." I can say this only to people who know what they want. One of the things I often ask people when I have this kind of discussion is this: "What really gives you kicks and joy and a glow?" Another question I ask them is "What drives you?" Because if you look at the difference between drive and satisfaction, you can understand an awful lot.

Townsend: The phrase I use to describe what you're talking about is "do what makes your heart leap." And if your heart doesn't leap when you're at a job, for heaven's sake, don't stay.

Bennis: It all starts with the initial job interview. You've got to recruit with scrupulous honesty. You've really got to tell people what they're getting into so that they're not going to be trapped in a false dream. You've got to recruit in a way that's congruent with the goals and visions of the institution.

Townsend: Once at American Express, I was asked to start a credit card. I demurred. I said, "I refuse to start the credit card, but I'll find somebody." And they said, "Why won't you run it?" And I said, "Because it demands expertise in machine accounting and I know I don't have that experience. But worse than that, you'll never give me a moment's peace. But I'll find you somebody." Well, I found that person. I used a search firm, went outside, didn't promote from within, because we had nobody remotely near what we needed to start a new business.

I had a long talk with him. I told him how much to ask for, because this was an organization that underpaid everybody. I knew what he should be getting and I knew what the company was going to offer him and it wasn't enough.

I told him to insist on locating himself twenty-five blocks away so he wouldn't ever be available to the chief executive officer, who otherwise would have had him in a waiting room half his life. The organization would have failed because he was in the CEO's waiting room instead of running the business. I told him to run the business as if he owned it and take wild and crazy chances and see if he could get through three years without being fired and bring the company into the black. And I told him to pay no attention whatsoever to what anybody else in the company said to him. He wouldn't be reporting to me, but I said, "This is my coaching to you before you go into the company."

He took all of my advice. He did bring it into the black within three years. He located way uptown. He never saw the CEO, except at quarterly meetings. And he did a great job.

Dialogue Starters

1. DEBATE QUESTION: Is there any gender or racial bias present at your company? What, if anything does leadership do about this? Do you feel there should be a written policy on these issues? Why or why not?

2. ROLE-PLAYING DIALOGUE: Have your partner pretend to be looking for a job. You pretend to be the interviewer. Decide what it means to "recruit with honesty" and practice doing so with your partner. What difficulties do you encounter when interviewing this way? Do you believe in this form of interviewing? Why or why not? Do you see how it might improve job performance? Why or why not?

How do you go about choosing a leader for the top spot in an organization?

Townsend: You ask yourself, "Is there anything I can do at this meeting to make sure we are considering all the candidates that should be considered before the board picks a doppelgänger or a clone of the outgoing CEO?"

Bennis: Which happens too often.

Townsend: I raise the question because I think it's at the root of one of our biggest problems, which is why we keep putting the wrong kinds of people in the corner office. And why our organizations, as we agree, are generally badly led and people are frustrated in them, when they don't have to be frustrated if we can solve this one problem, or at least shed some light on it. One of the things I would do if I were in that meeting as an inside director is say, "I am not a candidate, so you can assume what I say is objective and not self-serving. I think we ought to consider people from three levels, from three layers of the company. Not just consider the people in this room or the people reporting to the people in this room, but the people below that." Then get a broad list of candidates and look at their records and talk to the people who work for them, interview them, get a sense of their vision for the company and their satisfaction or dissatisfaction with the status quo and open up a much broader list. Because we want to be sure that we've considered as broad a list as possible in our search for the person who's going to lead us for the next five or ten years.

Bennis: The thing that gets us into trouble is the logic of the obvious choice. Because the logic of the obvious choice is usually the clone, the doppelgänger. Your response to your own question is to really do a thorough analysis and surface as much as you can the challenges that are facing that organization in the next five to ten years. And to see whether or not the people within that inside group—incidentally, even three layers down you might not get the right person—but to see to what extent the fit works.

When I've called people about whether so-and-so might be a decent candidate, the real question is, for what? I want to make sure that the situation we're going to be confronting, the challenges we're going to be dealing with and addressing, are those that our pool of candidates can deal with. I'm not always sure that's true, because the CEO often has too much influence on the board in these matters and tends to favor the clones. Because most leaders, my experience is, tend to choose people who are like them instead of people who compensate for their deficiencies.

I've noticed two kinds of leaders, those who pick people who are reflectors and those who are compensators. The compensators say, "I want to choose people who can make up for what I'm not good at." I don't find enough of those. I find too many people who seek their clones or doppelgängers.

Townsend: Related to that, I think, is a necessity for the leader to enjoy the business and to have respect for the business and to love working in it, a lot like Roger Milliken, who's still working as an older man and is still a respected leader in his industry. He loves the business. Genevieve Gore is another executive who's still working, and loves the business.

Bennis: You've really got to love it. But in order to love it, I think you really have to know the business. Too often you find these managers who alternate between just being financial experts and knowing when to divest or invest, and managing, but that's not leadership. That's dancing to the joy of numbers and using business-ese that makes you sound important.

Townsend: And they can't survive the energy requirements, and I mean personal energy requirements, of leadership unless they love the business. That means they love the suppliers and they love the employees and they love the customers and they just can't wait to get to the office in the morning. I think that's a requirement.

Bennis: It's interesting, the only question I had a hard time answering about my university days as president was when I was giving a lecture at Harvard and the dean of the School of Education, Paul Ylvisaker, asked me a question that just stumped me. I was blocked; I couldn't answer the question. He said, "Do you love the university enough?" He could tell from the melancholy tone in my voice, when I talked about trying to fight the bureaucracy, that I wasn't loving it as much as I should. I was about a year or two away from leaving the university. I didn't know that, then.

What would you advise an executive? And the advice doesn't have to be for the CEO, but any manager. What advice would you give about coping with the stress and the hard work?

Townsend: Well, my reaction to the question of what to do with burnout applies to the whole spectrum of organizations. We have to have a provision of either sabbatical luxuries to recharge the batteries and then come back into a different job, or retirement or semiretirement luxuries. A vice-chairman can take over a public relations function for the company and make all the speeches and attend all the

Red Cross and local hospital fund drives and chair all the outside boards.

Bennis: And after you've removed the PR people you're going to put in this successfully burned-out CEO to run the PR Department.

Townsend: No, there's no department. He's it. And he's not allowed to hire anybody.

Bennis: I see. . . .

Townsend: It's him and his secretary who run public relations. What we want to do is recharge him. But, unfortunately, what we often do is inundate the CEO with luxuries and distractions at the moment he's picking up the torch. It's like tossing him into a swimming pool with the torch and wondering why it goes out.

Bennis: I want to add a few things to this discussion about recharging your employees because I love the idea. And the one thing I like about the university is this notion of sabbaticals, although I think they ought to have them more frequently and for shorter periods of time.

John Sculley, former CEO of Apple Computer, once took about three months off. He went to an island off Maine and didn't even have a fax machine. He reconfigured the whole idea of what Apple was about during that eleven-week respite. He thought about how much longer he wanted to stay, and rethought the whole company.

Ken Olsen, the head of Digital, goes off every summer on a canoe trip with about six friends. None of them are from Digital. They go away for about ten days. When Nan Keohane, one of my favorite university administrators, was the head of Wellesley (she's now president of Duke), she took off a full year. She went out to Stanford and thought a lot for a year. She asked her dean of college to be interim president for a year. She came back totally reinspired and repotted.

I would also recommend every executive keep a journal, to take time for reflection, which is what a sabbatical is all about. And to get away from the present, because the present is always "too present" when you're a CEO. I think it helps enormously to have an opportunity to reflect.

It's real important in the character of a leader not to let self-esteem be based solely on that position. Basing your self-esteem only on your job can be deadly. My predecessor at the university that I presided over for a number of years died after he retired, and a lot of other leaders, by the way, either have heart attacks or die very quickly after they give up their positions. So I don't know how you'd instruct people about that, but there ought to be outlets for joy and fun other than just work.

Dialogue Starters

1. LISTING EXERCISE: Make a list of all the steps the people at your company take to choose a leader. Do they pick only from the top of the hierarchy or would you say they select a broad cross section of people? Now list all the qualities you think they look for in a leader. Then list all the qualities you think are important to look for in a leader. Where do the two lists intersect? Based on what you know about your company, who do you think is likely to be chosen next? How can you make a positive impact on the selection process?

2. MANAGEMENT EVALUATION: How often do your management people take time off from their duties? Do you feel they (or you) keep themselves refreshed with new ideas

and continually demonstrate interest in the company? Do they encourage a balanced lifestyle or do they prefer that people spend most of their time in the office? What effect does this have on the rest of the workers? What is the company policy on sabbaticals? Is this a good time to change the policy?

Chapter 11

Forging Leaders

In a successful work environment that's stimulating and energizing, people are empowered to work better and to achieve more. Leaders help followers to lead themselves.

In this chapter, you'll learn how to grow leadership in the ranks—how to be what we call a "leader grower." Leader growers are able to earn the trust and respect of their followers by helping others to develop in their careers. They practice techniques that promote leadership rather than inhibit it. And when they have done their job well, they are rewarded by seeing the people they have grown move on to better positions with more responsibility.

If you're in the process of becoming the new leader discussed in this book, you're already building *other leaders who can play special roles in transforming your organization. Growing other leaders from the ranks isn't just a* duty *of the leader, it's an* obligation.

One of the best kinds of leader growers is the mentor. Many good leaders foster this kind of special relationship, and for the emerging leader, it's best to seek mentors early on. There is an art to choosing the right mentor and developing a "sponsorship" system to learn the most in any job situation.

—WARREN BENNIS

How can a leader grow other leaders?

Townsend: I have something to say to a follower and how a follower becomes a leader. A follower has to make up her mind that she's going to live by Judeo-Christian principles.

Now that sounds corny, but let's say she's lost down as a galley slave in the organization somewhere; maybe she has just been assigned five people to report to her in some arcane subbasement. That's when she says, "I'm going to help others. I'm going to see how much my five people can earn, instead of how little I can pay them. I'm going to earn their respect and their trust. I'm going to do what I can to understand what they want to get out of the organization. If it means they leave me when they're the most valuable players I've got on my team, I'm going to move heaven and earth to get them moved. And if they all get promoted above me, I will consider myself a thundering success. I will keep on doing that and expect that if I do it well enough and twenty-five people who used to work for me have become vice-presidents, someday somebody's going to tap me on the shoulder and say, 'We have a more interesting job for you to do.' "

Bennis: I don't know of one institution that I've talked with, and I think I've talked to at least the top three hundred companies in this country, that rewards people for developing leaders—and there's no incentive for me to want to give up people who are doing a super job. I want to keep them.

Townsend: I wish the English language were better, but we ought to have a category for the people who raise leaders and create leaders and never get promoted or moved themselves. Call them leader growers and make it a very major title with major rewards.

Bennis: Do we have any better language? Is there any word for that? *Coach* isn't it. *Mentor* isn't it. *Leader grower* is, with all due respect, Bob, kind of a clumsy phrase.

Townsend: No. . . .

Bennis: But I don't know, we ought to invent a word.

Townsend: Well, I just invented the word, and you told me it was no good.

Bennis: It's sort of clumsy.

Townsend: See, now you hurt my ego. . . .

Bennis: Lots of people ask me what recommendations or advice I would give to a CEO, the social architect of an organization, in order for that person to grow more leadership or to create better leadership development. And I think there are several things that ought to be considered. Those factors that promote and those factors that inhibit the growth of leadership. And let me just talk to each of those questions.

One of the first things you've got to remember, for new employees especially, is to give them challenging assignments early in a career, because too often the first jobs they get are the most boring, narrow, and constricted jobs.

And if you don't, people get ossified very early in their careers. But if you stretch people and help them grow in many dimensions, I think you've got one leg up on growing leaders.

The second thing is to give them as much exposure as possible to many role models, because people learn as much from bad leaders as they do from good leaders. The more the merrier. The more people who can look at different leaders and observe, the better it is for their own growth. Research by M. W. McCall and others indicates that people learn more from bosses who are in some ways extreme in their behavior.[1]

It's when the relationship is so easy and the boss is really easygoing that people don't learn. Bosses who are extreme force employees to stretch in all kinds of ways. And the more of those visible role models employees can come in contact with, the better.

Third, assign a person to head up a task force. But not just one of those meaningless task forces that we often do to decide on the color of the wallpaper or the size of offices. A really significant task force that is highly visible and relevant to the goals of the organization. Put those people in charge of a group where they do not have a hierarchical authority over them—where there are people above them in status and people below them in status and people at their own level. And put them in the spotlight. In that situation, those people are going to learn an enormous amount. In other words, keep testing, keep risking, keep

1. For more information, see M. W. McCall, M. M. Lombardo, and A. W. Morrison, *The Lessons of Experience* (New York: Lexington Books, 1988).

stretching people—"stretch," as coaches say, not strain. That's the kind of an organization that grows leaders.

What inhibits leadership is another series of moves that too many organizations make. One is they give people a long series of narrow, tactical jobs. So they make short-term and tactically oriented decisions and never develop long-run or strategic kinds of goals.

The second thing that inhibits leadership is making only vertical career movement. One of the things that the best organizations I know of do consistently is a lot of horizontal movement. The Japanese, by the way, are terrific at this. But if you look at Glaxo, which is the largest pharmaceutical company in the world, or Arco, before you can get to the top of that organization, you have to play a vital role in every single one of the divisions within it. You have to be in the research lab, you have to be a salesperson, you have to work in planning, you have to be in manufacturing, you have to be in distribution—there's not one significant function of Glaxo that you don't have to participate in before you can move to any top-level job in the organization. You see, the problem with vertical movement alone— vertical movement might be OK if job A prepared you for job B and job B prepared you for job C. But organizations aren't that rational and they're not that linear. Take finance as an example. At the lowest levels of finance you're a bookkeeper or a cop. Up at the top, you're involved in legitimate gambling. There are totally different kinds of requirements for these jobs.

Townsend: You've got to get very specific, it seems to me, on how long people stay in these horizontal moves, because some sharp CEO will come in and say, "Oh boy, I'll just switch people for six months into new jobs," and what they do is more damage than good.

Bennis: I totally agree with that. As a matter of fact, I was getting to that in my next point about what inhibits leadership, which is a premature promotion. Movement that is too rapid is another way of putting it. But that does not help people to think long term or to learn the impact of their actions over the long term. And also, premature promotions or just moving people around too quickly can encourage a kind of manipulative style.

And finally, another inhibitor is measurements and rewards based only on short-term performance, which is exactly what we want to get rid of. That method of evaluation encourages people to pay attention to the management aspects of their jobs and ignore the leadership aspects.

Those are the things I would watch out for, if I were the social architect, if I were giving advice to leaders, if I were giving advice to you about what to do to create an environment that would nourish and grow leaders.

Townsend: But don't write any memos about it. Just do it. You don't have to write a three-page memo, or, even worse, have your Human Resources Department write a ten-page Leatherette-bound document on cross-training. If you want to put an organization to sleep, that's the way to do it.

Bennis: Who reads those anyway but the people who write them?

Townsend: Exactly.

Dialogue Starters

1. DEFINITION EXERCISE: **Define all the ways your organization tries to promote leadership qualities in its employ-**

ees. Define three things you can do personally to develop leaders in your department. Define three ways you think management can improve in its ability to grow leaders in your department or other departments.

2. WHAT-IF DISCUSSION: What if management called all the employees together to tell them they've decided to give lateral promotions? That means, instead of making a move up the ladder, everyone would just move to a different position in the company. How would that benefit the company? How would it hinder the company? What if this policy were implemented every few years, so that it occurred twice in a decade? Would it change the way you interview prospective employees? Would it change how you measure contribution and performance? How so? Do you think it would increase company loyalty? Would workers want to expand their skills or would they resent losing their familiar positions?

How can we encourage people to grow leaders?

Bennis: For one thing, we have got to start identifying potential leaders and taking a look at them, and then figuring out ways of rewarding them. Because sometimes it turns out that the really good coaches may not themselves be the best leaders. The best tennis coaches aren't necessarily the best players. Certainly in baseball, very few of the greatest coaches have ever been anything but sort of decent minor-league players.

What organizations have to do first is recognize who these people are, and start really rewarding them, celebrating them, putting up their hall of fame. That's a very simple thing, though I don't know of any organization that does it.

Townsend: I don't either. It's not too hard to just look around and see who's losing leaders to other companies and whose people are getting promoted. The leader grower may be overlooked because she doesn't look very prepossessing, isn't too articulate, or whatever. Or she may not be someone who attracts attention.

Bennis: Yes.

Townsend: And in an environment where risk taking and creativity are rewarded, everybody comes to work excited. People work crazy hours; there's lots of energy, lots of mistakes; they all feel zap-proof and they're having fun. It doesn't matter what the leader grower's profile is. If that's happening in the office and she's in charge, she's a leader grower. That's all you need to know, and all you need to look for in an organization. Where is that kind of excitement going on? No organization's going to stop that from happening. I mean, they all recognize someone who is taking risks, as you said, and they ask for this kind of risk-taking behavior and wish it would happen more. So if someone does behave that way, they generally tolerate it.

Bennis: I thought I was very lucky in having the mentors I did. But I realized later I was very active, even proactive, in choosing them. I didn't just wait around to be selected. I went out of my way to say, "I really want to work with Doug McGregor. I really want to work with Abe Maslow. I really want to work with Carl Rogers." I was able to corner some of the great minds, and I was active about it. And that's the first thing I would say about carving out a career in any profession. I'm not just talking about business, but

I'm talking about any single profession—work with the best people you possibly can.

Townsend: You were an active, articulate, intelligent, interested . . .

Bennis: Go on.

Townsend: . . . Ph.D. in what was then called behavioral science, and you could get to Maslow.

Bennis: Yes.

Townsend: You could get to McGregor, you could get to Carl Rogers. Suppose somebody says, "I want to work for Jack Welch." How the devil does he get to work for GE, and if he does, how does he get Jack Welch's attention, which is what he went there for in the first place?

Bennis: Well, in the GE situation, I would say, "Who are the rising stars from whom I could learn the most?" I would go after some of the younger people whose career seems to be going up and from whom I think I could learn an awful lot, and see how I could somehow get connected with them. We have to seed organizations not just with one leader grower, but I guess we have to have as many of them as we can.

Townsend: The thing that I've always felt I'd do if I had to do it over again, so that I could learn the most from my work experience, is try to work for a small company for a couple of years, and then the largest company I could find for a couple of years. Never mind whether they are great companies full of mentors or the worst companies in the world. As you pointed out, maybe the worst company in the world would be a great learning place.

Now, this brings us back to the Gore company. The only way you and I could join the Gore company would be to find an associate to sponsor us. You have a sponsor when you begin work there who watches your progress for ninety days. Along with the other people you've dealt with, the sponsor decides at the end of ninety days whether you're an associate or whether you're let go. Once you're in there as an associate, you're free to pick other people as sponsors if they'll agree. So you could have two or three sponsors in the company to consult with or with whom you can discuss opportunities or ideas. And finally, in the Gore system, leaders are defined as "the people you turn to when you need help." In that kind of outfit, which Bill Gore described as a "lattice organization," you have a multiplicity of people to go to.

Bennis: I like that. There are a lot of other companies that are perhaps not as highly evolved as Gore, but companies like Arthur Little or many other consulting firms work like Gore does. You've got a project; you get excited about it; people like to work with you because they know you've had successful projects and they're going to learn from you— from the leader. I think this situation develops followers sort of spontaneously rather than through the structural approach—you know, when you report to that person who is excited about the work. I'd like to see more organizations structured the way Gore is, with cross-functional projects and people who work together intensely.

Dialogue Starters

1. Brainstorming Dialogue: Can you brainstorm a few ways that organizations can recognize and reward leader growers? What about in your organization? Can you think of ways followers might be able to nominate leader grow-

ers for promotion? What about a Leader Grower of the Year award?

2. DEFINITION EXERCISE: What's the difference between a leader grower and a mentor? Between a good mentor and a not-so-good mentor? Do you believe in seeking out mentors in your organization? What about outside your organization? Give an example of the best way to ask for mentoring. How would you like to be approached?

Chapter 12

Choosing a Leader

Leaders. They manage themselves, inspire others, and forge the future. They are full of questions and wary of easy answers. They explore and dream and are tireless believers in people. They are willing to take risks and are committed to excellence—along with readiness, virtue, and vision. Leaders strive to face things as they are and prepare for things as they will be. If you believe that competence and conscience must be restored, you must demonstrate both.

In this chapter, you'll learn "the Bennis test" and "the Townsend test" for leadership selection. You'll learn why it's important to find someone who is ambitious and capable, but not too ambitious and capable, in your organization. You'll also learn the importance of consulting others whom the potential leaders work with, before making your final choices. Finally, we'll offer a couple of key points to remember when practicing the art of leadership.

—ROBERT TOWNSEND

How do you choose a leader?

Townsend: There are generally four kinds of people that you have to choose from when you choose a leader.

The first is the overly ambitious type—always attracting attention, a brownnoser, frequently successful in getting promoted. The absolute worst choice in the company. This type of person wants power, needs power, and can't live without power. He is authoritarian, insensitive, and careless of others. Always ask the question about this person, "Will this candidate help get people excited and energetic and creative in pursuit of company goals?" Ask his peers and his subordinates—eyeball to eyeball—about how it is to work with him and for him.

The second is the scientist or professional devoted to her field and working in the organization. She has no time for administrative hassle, and wouldn't even take the job. If she does take it, she won't be good at it.

Then there's the excellent, dependable nine-to-fiver whose priorities are family first, then outside interests, and finally the job. Very good from nine to five, but his heart won't be in it as a leader, which is an eighty-hour-a-week job and would change his whole life.

Fourth is the intelligent person who is not overly ambitious. She can easily live without power. She's respected by all who have to deal with her. She won't really jump up and down. This person will say, "Somebody's got to do it, so I'll try." This last type of leader will be very good, the best choice.

Bennis: I've been developing a set of questions that I'd like to ask job candidates or potential leaders. I don't have all that much faith in psychological tests, but there are certain sets of questions that I think would be quite useful in understanding and perhaps making a better choice of the leaders we do select. Here are some examples: Tell me about a time when you've tried to help someone else change. What strategy did you use? How did it turn out? Tell me about your most challenging or least challenging job. Tell me about a time when you had to overcome major obstacles to meet a challenge. Tell me about the people you most and least admire. Tell me about a time when you tried to do something but failed. Tell me about a time when something bad happened to you. Tell me about a mistake you made in dealing with people. Tell me about the last time you made a major change—why did you do it? How did it work out?

Now we can all think of decent questions. I would also add that there are five criteria that most organizations use to evaluate people: technical competence, people skills, conceptual skills, judgment, and character. And incidentally, it is almost always the last two criteria that companies rely on, whether or not they admit it. I've never seen anyone not get a top job because of a lack of technical competence. Sometimes it's people skills but most often it's judgment and character.

Townsend: We're talking about corporations and business entities, not entrepreneurs or small businesses. And I'm assuming that the candidates who are being asked these questions have all served in the organization; they're not outsiders. My first set of questions would be: What dissatisfies you about this organization? What would be high on your priority list to try to change? Give me your vision of where you'd like this organization, not you personally, to be five years from now. Finally, give me a rough idea of how you plan to go about accomplishing it.

If anybody's a serious candidate and has worked ten years, let's say, in the organization, and if she doesn't have a vision of where it ought to be five years from now, that person's not a candidate. She's seen everything that she hates, everything that she can't stand, all the people that she thinks are headed in the wrong direction. If you give her twenty-four hours to think about the question, that person should be able to give you a good answer.

When we talk about choosing a leader, I would talk to everybody who works as a peer with these candidates and everybody who is subordinate to and who has to work for these people and just say, "What's your view? How are they? How is it to work for them?" There is no need to get too personal. You don't have to say, "Should we promote?" Obviously, that's in everybody's mind, but just say, "How is it to work with them or work for them?" I think if you're persistent and ask enough people, you'll get a pretty clear picture of who are the leaders and who are the tyrants.

Is this someone who puts the blame on his organization when anything goes wrong? Or is this someone who protects his people from blame? Do they think he walks on water? Or do they think he's an unreliable, absent, invisible, miserable character who's gotten to the top by misleading the management? You can find all these things out if you talk to enough of the people.

Bennis: Perhaps what's missing from that list, though, is one major factor. What's lacking is integrity and some kind of a moral, ethical stance and centeredness. And that's the one, perhaps, that you could pick up most of all from talking to people's direct reports. I don't like the word *subordinates*. How about *followers?*

Townsend: *Peers.*

Bennis: *Peers,* yes, that's good.

Townsend: If you get enough feedback from this group that says "He's slippery," or "You better get it in writing," you can almost cross that candidate off the list.

Bennis: What I was going to say is that you can get only a certain amount out of a personal interview. I do think an interview is important, but not sufficient.

The questions that both you and I are raising, in my view, are basically methods and means and avenues for getting at the candidates' capacity to learn, how they deal with complexity, how they recognize ambiguity, how curious they are. Do they have analytical honesty and a degree of self-awareness? Those qualities are what I think both of us are looking for. And these characteristics are, in some implicit way, what I look for in friends as well as colleagues—not just leaders.

What I'm interested in is the reflective practitioner. A person who can really think, act, and make things happen. Someone who keeps learning and moving in that direction. I don't think you learn without acting. If you really want to learn about something, try to change it. That's why one of the questions I'd ask is "Tell me about an experience you've had where you've tried to change a system or change a person." Because that's how I really think you understand. You don't understand by just observing it. You have to try to change it. That would be the Bennis test.

Townsend: Listen, I respect your position on this and I think history may prove how right you are in trying to get people with integrity into the CEO's office, which is what you're trying to do. But having said that, I'll remind you of what I've said before, which is the Townsend test.

You pick someone who wants the job, but not too much. You pick someone who has the respect of subordinates and peers in the area where she has recently worked and worked even before that. You pick someone who looks like 50 percent of what you were hoping for and you give her the job. And all the people who have worked around her and under her before will rally to help her make up the additional 50 percent, because they perceive that she earned a shot at the job.

The reason you pick someone in the organization who looks like 50 percent of what you were hoping for is that you don't get to look like more than 50 percent if you're a loyal and dedicated follower. You don't try to shine and show how ready you are to put your boss out to pasture. It's not nice, it's not productive, it's not healthy, it's not the way you deal with your colleagues and peers—to try to make yourself look better than they are. So everybody sort of plays it cool. If you can find people who are well respected, who look like 50 percent, they're already at 90 percent in competence. If the organization is supportive of them, they'll grow in no time at all.

Maybe we should add, develop a statement of the rough challenges of the next ten years; get a list of ten people within the company from at least three levels and then look objectively at which one you'd rather have leading the company for the next five to seven years.

Bennis: I would add to that one other thing. I would like to see a couple of really powerful external stakeholders join that group, not just the people within. I would also like to see some of the firm's major customers participate in that group. I think that mix of people would be terrific, and I don't know of any case where they do that.

Townsend: No, I don't either. I think it's an excellent idea.

Dialogue Starters

1. MANAGEMENT EVALUATION: Examine those you work for as well as those who work for you. Which of the four types of leadership styles do they possess? Are they:

• The Authoritarian
• The Scientist
• The Dependable Nine-to-fiver
• The Intelligent but Not Overly Ambitious Type

How do their styles affect their effectiveness as leaders? As followers? Which is your style? Determine how changing your style of leadership might affect those with whom and for whom you work.

2. DEFINITION EXERCISE: Review the qualities of leadership that, as Warren Bennis calls him, a "reflective practitioner" possesses. What qualities would you add to this definition? How easy is change within your organization? Could a reflective practitioner do a good job there?

If there were one or two basic points about leadership you'd like to make, what would they be?

Bennis: I'll tell you the points that come to my mind. People, to coin an old phrase, are the key and only significant thing that really counts in an organization. Basically the technology's going to be pretty even among competitors, but the competitive edge is clearly people and their leadership. That's one of the fundamentals.

Louis B. Mayer, known as a tyrant, once said something really interesting. He said, "You know, in this Hollywood scene and making films, it's all people. That's the only cost we have. In fact, they're my inventory. And," he said, "my inventory goes home at night."

The second thing that you and I really agree on, and I think is a fundamental, is that you can't manage people. You can't tell people how to be self-aware. Everything we've talked about has to do with people really doing it for themselves. You can manage yourself. I'm not so confident about managing others. We can inspire, we can generate, we can open doors, we can reward, but, by God, if there's anything we've focused on, it is the celebration of the individual in making the difference.

You have a meeting with your group weekly. Suppose you say, "We're going to have an extra half hour at this meeting, and I want you to think about several questions and answer them either here or at the next meeting. What are we doing wrong here? What should we be doing? What should we become in five years? What's wrong with this organization as it stands now? Have we got the right people? Are they properly compensated? What excuses do they have for not doing the best work in our industry or in this particular field?'' And if that doesn't light up some eyes, I don't know what will. And that's the process that you can do without talking to anybody—without writing any memos—you can just start thinking. Get your organization thinking about what we want to become and how we get there.

That's the final Bennis/Townsend principle, which is bias toward action. It's that everything you've got to do, everything you want to do, has to be sustained, tried through action.

I recently attended a marriage conducted by a rabbi, and he gave a beautiful speech. The thing I most remember from the speech was a story he told that took place in prerevolutionary Russia back at the turn of the century. A rabbi is walking over to the synagogue and he is stopped by a Russian soldier. With his rifle at forward arms, the soldier says gruffly, ''Who are you and what are you doing here?'' The rabbi says, ''How much do they pay you for doing this job?'' The soldier says, ''Twenty kopecks.'' Then the rabbi says, ''I'll pay you twenty-five kopecks if every day you stop me right here and ask me those two questions.''

This philosophy is what we've been talking a lot about. We can prompt the questions, but you've got to do the answering.

Townsend: What are you doing here and are you . . .

Bennis: Who are you and what are you doing here?

Townsend: And are you having fun yet?

The 21-Day Plan

Now that you've read *Reinventing Leadership,* you are equipped with all of the information and answers you need to become an effective, inspiring leader. However, you still might not be completely prepared to assume that role. While we have given you plenty of information, practical application is still required.

That's why we've created this 21-Day Plan. It will help you apply what you have learned about being an effective leader. Besides pen and paper, all you need is some time every day to tackle a new section of this plan. Then, at the end of three weeks, return to the first section and compare what you have learned with what you already knew. We believe that you will see a dramatic change in your ability to function as a strong leader.

Day One

To begin, consider what your own personal answers are to the four important questions that follow, questions that are central to being both a well-defined individual and an effective leader. Really take time to think about these questions. Do a little digging into your heart and your mind. Consider your present realities, as well your hopes and your dreams. Measure your strengths and your current weaknesses before answering the questions.

Throughout the next three weeks, keep these questions in mind and make changes in your responses as they are warranted. Be in touch with these changes and with the events or stimuli—both internal and external—that create them. Remember, truly effective leaders know themselves as well as or better than those whom they lead.

Who are you?

_____

_____

_____

What are you doing here?

_____

_____

_____

Whom do you *want* to be?

_____

_____

_____

What do you *want* your purpose to be?

_____

_____

_____

Day Two

A business short of capital can borrow money. One with a poor location can move. But a business—or any organization—short on leadership has little chance of survival. Too often, people overmanage and underlead. Short-term profit is their only vision. Innovation loses out to the bottom line.

Because a new breed of leadership is needed to refocus and reshape organizations so they'll thrive into the next century, leaders should be women and men who understand that leadership is essentially a human business, who believe that the quality of life for everyone is improved when leadership is put into action, and who use their commitment, convictions, and constituencies for the greater good.

*   *   *

On a scale of 1–5 (1 being the lowest, 5 the highest), rate how much of each of the following traits you currently possess. Answer as honestly as you can. Remember, your answers should reflect where you are now. You can return to this section in the future and reevaluate yourself each time as your evolution as a leader and a person continues.

Ambition/drive	1	2	3	4	5
Expertise	1	2	3	4	5
Integrity	1	2	3	4	5
Vision	1	2	3	4	5
Purpose	1	2	3	4	5
Effectiveness	1	2	3	4	5

Select at least two items above on which you scored yourself low. Determine why you believe yourself to be weak in these areas. Think of at least three specific actions you can take to help yourself become stronger in these areas.

Day Three

Because executive character is marked by three characteristics that act as the three legs of a tripod—constructive ambition, competent expertise, and consistent values—it is important that the three are not only developed but also brought into balance.

Just as a tripod with one leg too short, too long, or missing is unable to stand firmly or function properly, a leader with one of the required traits underdeveloped, overdeveloped, or missing is a leader who is flawed—perhaps fatally so.

One of the three aspects of executive character is maintaining consistent values, but it is too often surprising and discouraging how many people can't say exactly what their values are. Do you know what you believe in? On a piece of paper, quickly list a half-dozen things about which you feel passionately and for which you stand.

Now, put a check mark next to each of the items you've listed that is consistently reflected in your actions. In other words, identify the values and beliefs you display when you walk your talk.

For any of the values that you were unable to put a check mark next to—values you act contrary to—write down any specific instances in which you did not act on your beliefs. Were you aware of them when they were happening? How did it feel? How do you feel about it now?

List any specific actions you can take to bring your actions into closer alignment with your values and beliefs.

Day Four

Like beauty, leadership comes in many different forms. Among the many traits we discuss in this book are intelligence, humor, protectiveness, fairness, and decisiveness. But complicating our understanding and development of these and other traits is the appearance of apparently contradictory characteristics. For example, a leader is a person marked by both patience and a sense of urgency. He or she is someone who must be available, but not too available. Being an effective leader is nothing less than a balancing act. It is a matter of possessing varying traits, of knowing when each is needed, and of bringing each to the fore when it is needed and appropriate.

* * *

In the space provided, write out your personal description of what a leader is. You do not need to repeat attributes found in this book. Rather, based on your personal experience, your personal needs, and your preferences, create a definition that is a meaningful foundation on which you can build your own leadership skills.

_____

_____

_____

Day Five

If there is a single tip we would give to a man or woman aspiring to a leadership position, it is to get someone in his or her life who can be depended upon for reflective backtalk, i.e., reliable, responsible critiques and criticism of ideas and plans.

To encourage such reflective backtalk, to take a path that will eventually—and purposely—lead to disapproval, tests a leader's character and self-esteem. Remember that a true leader is not threatened by a difference of opinion; he or she welcomes it and seeks it out.

Answer the following questions true (T) or false (F):

a. I am confident of my ability to offer reflective backtalk in a constructive, nonthreatening manner.

   T _____   F _____

b. I consistently focus on a plan's advantages, not only its flaws.

   T _____   F _____

c. I am confident of my ability to accept reflective backtalk in an appreciative, nonthreatened manner.

T _____   F _____

d. I consistently accept feedback and criticism graciously and gratefully.

T _____   F _____

e. I currently have at least one person in my life to whom I give reflective backtalk.

T _____   F _____

f. I currently have at least one person in my life from whom I receive reflective backtalk.

T _____   F _____

What dangers do you see in giving or receiving reflective backtalk? How can these dangers be avoided? Do you have a system in place for evaluating criticism, creative dissent, and contradictory ideas? Can you devise one that avoids the dangers and downsides you have listed?

Day Six

Without a point of view, where are you? Without a vision, where's the meaning?

Vision can be described as many things, but basically it is a sense of knowing what you want. Yet that sense, that vision, is useless unless it is clearly articulated to everyone in an organization and, more important, acted upon. A vision must always be sustained by cogent, consistent organizational action.

Leaders have a vision. They communicate their vision to the people around them in ways that are emotionally engaging, making these people stakeholders in the vision and its success.

In the space that follows, write down the vision you have for your organization. It is vital that you are able to describe your vision clearly and succinctly to yourself—for if you can't communicate it to yourself, how can you communicate it to others?

———————————————————————

———————————————————————

———————————————————————

Day Seven

Leaders are the most results-oriented people in the world. This fixation with and attention to outcome is possible only if a person knows what he or she wants. Knowing what you want and being able to translate it into action are the two keys to effective leadership.

- On a sheet of paper, list a single, short-term goal for your organization that will begin to move the organization toward your vision.
- In what ways can you communicate that goal to others in your organization?

- In what specific ways can you measure progress made toward that goal?
- How will you reward this progress?
- Are there any obstacles interfering with your goal, including jobs or departments not necessary to the outcome?

Day Eight

Leaders invent themselves; they don't contrive. They learn to put themselves together, make themselves their own creations. People who are going to become leaders are going to have to make up their minds that they must change themselves—and that they are not going to get much help from others.

No one else can teach you how to become yourself, to take charge, to express yourself. Only you can do that. Remember the four lessons of self-knowledge: You are your own best teacher; accept responsibility, blame no one; you can learn anything you want to learn; and true understanding comes from reflecting on your experiences.

What do you need to learn to improve yourself *professionally*?

_____

_____

_____

How can you go about getting this education? What tools and teachers do you need?

_____

_____

_____

What will you do with this new knowledge?

_____

_____

_____

What do you need to learn to improve yourself *personally?*

_____

_____

_____

Day Nine

Leaders can't order people to trust them. Trust is earned. It must be a synergistic relationship existing throughout an organization, at all levels—trusting down, trusting up, trusting sideways.

For each of the following Four Cs of trust, rate yourself on a scale of 1–5 (1 being the lowest, 5 the highest) on the amount of each you possess.

Competence	1	2	3	4	5
Congruity	1	2	3	4	5
Caring	1	2	3	4	5
Consistency	1	2	3	4	5

In the space that follows, write the name of one person you totally trust, professionally or personally. Beneath that person's name, write the qualities he or she possesses that have created that trust in you. Finally, put a check mark to the right of each of the qualities you share with that person.

Name: _____

Qualities: _____ _____

_____ _____

_____ _____

_____ _____

_____ _____

_____ _____

Day Ten

One very important way in which leaders can earn the trust of the men and women they lead is by listening. Although this may sound simple enough, listening is a skill that few people have actually mastered.

Listening to what people have to say—whether or not the leader agrees with what is being said—is how a leader shows others that he or she cares about their point of view.

It is also an invaluable way to learn about areas of an organization usually unexplored and often overlooked by a leader. And it is a way to promote understanding among all members of an organization.

In the space that follows, record your thoughts on your listening abilities. What kind of listener are you? What are your strong points? What are your weaknesses? What specifically can you do to improve your listening skills? Can you recall a specific incident that illustrates areas in which your listening abilities can be improved?

Day Eleven

One of a leader's duties—and greatest joys—is to foster the growth of his or her people, to enjoy and encourage their development. The goal is to create an empowered work force, for when people feel significant, capable, and trusted they feel they are part of a community. This can lead only to better quality and greater innovation in the workplace.

A leader begins developing this empowered work force by being a role model to those around him or her, by displaying the attributes desired in staff members or colleagues. In order to do this, the four most important things a leader should be are: hopeful and optimistic, willing to take risks, honest, and understanding.

For each of the four characteristics, rate yourself on a scale of 1–5 (1 being the lowest, 5 the highest). Then, in the space provided, answer the following questions about how you've rated yourself for each characteristic: *Are you where you want to be on the scale? What can you do to improve in this area?*

Hopeful/optimistic   1   2   3   4   5

_____

_____

_____

Willing to take risks   1   2   3   4   5

_____

_____

_____

Honest   1   2   3   4   5

_____

_____

_____

Understanding	1	2	3	4	5

_____

_____

_____

Day Twelve

Delegation is also vital to leadership success. An extension of the idea of an organization as a cohesive team, delegation takes place only after identifying three things: what needs to be done, what people want to do, and what people are competent doing.

Finding capable men and women to take on new, more challenging tasks not only frees up the leader to concentrate on other details, but also creates and encourages the emergence of a new generation of leadership.

In some ways, delegating responsibility means giving up control, if only temporarily, of part of your job or part of your organization. How do you feel about relinquishing control? What are the benefits? What is the downside? Are there any unreasonable aspects in your responses to either of the last two questions?

If you were to delegate responsibility to someone on your staff, to whom would that delegation be made? Why do you feel that he or she is ready for increased responsibility? What part of your current responsibilities would you turn over? What would you do in the time you gained through delegation?

Day Thirteen

Taking risks and making your organizational world adapt to the changes a leader wants to make are, among many other things, tasks of that leader. Yet risk is not something taken lightly in most organizations, nor is the concept of change.

What is a leader to do?

It is the responsibility of a leader to activate a new paradigm, ACE—acknowledge, create, and empower—even if that means an entire organization must unlearn years of what, to most people, seems tried and true.

In the space that follows, detail how and why your present style is closer to the COP (control, order, predict) style or the ACE (acknowledge, create, empower) style.

_____

_____

_____

Whatever your answer to the previous question, what specifically can you do to become a person who leads even more consistently through acknowledgment, creativity, and empowerment?

_____

_____

_____

What are some ideas you have about the best ways to empower those people around you? Use the space provided for this brainstorming session.

_____

_____

_____

Day Fourteen

One of the surest ways to change an organization, to measure it, is through crisis. A company's vision is surely tested in a crisis—as are its people. If the vision holds up under fire, it becomes stronger and more meaningful to all stakeholders. Overcoming crises can also provide opportunities for doing things and solving problems in new ways—ways that will bring you closer to realizing the company vision.

An effective leader must learn to think kaleidoscopically. When he or she thinks of systems, it should not be of systems that confine. Rather, a leader must construct and believe in systems that are, essentially, partnerships. Hierarchies take away power; partnerships and teams empower.

Think of a recent crisis in your organization. What were its details? What made the situation become a crisis? How was the crisis handled?

How did your organization change as a result of the crisis? Are there other changes you believe should have come about as a result of it? Why didn't these changes occur?

How did you personally react to the crisis? How did you react to the resulting changes? How did they make you feel? Were you up to the challenge? How did you perform? What do you wish you'd done differently? What do you wish you'd done better?

Day Fifteen

There is an ongoing debate about whether a leader needs to be a specialist in his or her thinking and field, or whether general knowledge across a broad range is preferred. Ultimately, a leader's aim is to be a deep generalist—someone with a keen grasp of the details of a specific field, but also with the knowledge and ability to see and understand the bigger picture.

Are you a specialist or a generalist?

_____

What evidence can you provide to support your response?

_____

_____

_____

What specifically can you do to become more of a deep generalist?

_____

_____

_____

Day Sixteen

Moments when iron enters the soul of a leader, i.e., times of greatest failure, may be moments, too, of greatest learning.

A leader must be ready and willing to make mistakes, and he or she must be ready and willing for others to do the same. For it is only through our mistakes that we can create better ways of doing things.

How a leader handles his or her own mistakes, as well as the mistakes of others, speaks volumes about the way in which the organization will be run—and how it will succeed or fail.

What was the most recent error you made in your work?

_____

_____

_____

Did you admit your mistake? How? How did you feel?

_____

_____

_____

If you didn't admit your error, why not? What would have happened if you had?

_____

_____

_____

The last time a subordinate admitted a mistake, how did you react? Are you satisfied with that reaction?

_____

_____

_____

Whether or not you are happy with that reaction, what can you do the next time a subordinate admits an error to make your reaction a better, more constructive one?

_____

_____

_____

Day Seventeen

Casting blame on others can be habit forming. But it is a habit all leaders must break. If you tend to blame others for your own failures, you will never earn the respect of the men and women you must lead.

* * *

Use the space that follows to recall a time when you attempted to blame someone else for your own error.

_____

_____

_____

Were you successful in your attempt to blame someone else? Whether you were or not, how did you feel at that time?

_____

_____

_____

In retrospect, how do you now feel about your attempt?

_____

_____

_____

What specific actions can you take in the future to ensure that you are more able and willing to take responsibility for your own errors and actions?

_____

_____

_____

Day Eighteen

Language and cultural diversity, gender and color bias—these aren't new subjects in the world of business. In today's multicultural environment, a leader must be not only gender-blind, but also aware of racism and other personal biases. In this white-knuckle decade, human talent is too precious to disqualify people from your organization simply because of who or what they are.

Complete the following statements. In some instances, this may be an unpleasant experience, but we need to acknowledge and understand any beliefs and biases we hold before we can go about changing them. Be as honest as possible.

a. Male managers are: _____

b. Female managers are: _____

c. African-American managers are: _____

d. Caucasian managers are: _____

e. Hispanic managers are: _____

f. Asian managers are: _____

g. Catholic managers are: _____

h. Jewish managers are: _____

i. Fundamentalist Christian managers are: _____

j. Gay and lesbian managers are: _____

Day Nineteen

Unfortunately, this is an era of burnout, of seeking new challenges and considering new jobs. Leaders are constantly on the lookout for dissatisfaction—in others and in themselves. They combat and make provisions for burnout. Any individual is too valuable to lose through neglect.

In the space provided, use the left column to list possible signs and symptoms of burnout or job dissatisfaction. In the center column, write the names of any of the people you manage in whom you see any of these individual signs. Finally, in the right column, put a check next to any sign that you are aware of in yourself.

_____   _____   _____

_____   _____   _____

_____   _____   _____

_____   _____   _____

_____   _____   _____

_____   _____   _____

Day Twenty

There are four kinds of people from which to choose when looking for a leader—the overly ambitious, the scientist/professional, the dependable nine-to-fiver, and the intelligent, not overly ambitious person. Of the four, the last—intelligent, not overly ambitious—is the best choice for a leadership position. This is because someone of this type can easily live without power and, often because of that, is respected by all he or she would lead.

Of the four types of people listed above, into which category do you fall? Do you believe that an individual can span multiple categories? Do you feel that he or she can change categories over the course of a career? What might bring about that change?

Day Twenty-one

Becoming an effective, supportive, creative leader takes more than twenty-one days. It is an ongoing process that can span a career or a lifetime. But in the past twenty-one days you have been exposed to many of the pertinent issues at the very heart of leadership. You have confronted questions about yourself, how you act, and how you feel. You have taken important initial steps to improve your own leadership capabilities and those of others. And you have learned what it takes to develop future generations of corporate and social leaders.

Review this plan as frequently as you feel necessary, but certainly once every few months. Ask yourself the questions presented here more often than that. You answered some of the following questions on the very first first day of this 21-Day Plan. Do not be surprised if, because of your new knowledge and hard work, the answers to these questions are now somewhat different. The most vital perceptions and dreams are changeable things.

Who are you?

_____

_____

_____

How can you best communicate who you are to others?

_____

_____

_____

What are you doing here?

_____

_____

_____

What reasons can you give for the above response?

_____

_____

_____

Whom do you *want* to be?

_____

_____

_____

What goals can you set and what actions can you take to begin this transformation?

_____

_____

_____

What do you *want* your purpose to be?

_____

_____

_____

How will that help you and those around you to be better people and better leaders?

_____

_____

_____

Develop Your
Leadership Potential

Learn more new techniques for success by listening to Warren Bennis, Robert Townsend, and Tom Peters on audio programs available through Nightingale-Conant—the world's leading publisher of personal development programs.